contents

foreword	v
one	ix
one man	1
one world	15
one resolve	51
one child	85
one sponsor	109
one cause	125
one challenge	143
epilogue	156
notes	158

foreword

by Compassion President Wess K. Stafford, Ph.D.

Growing up as a missionary kid in a West African village, I often cried myself to sleep to the sound of beating drums, drums that signaled that one of my little playmates had died. By the time I was 15 years old, half the children I had begun my childhood with were gone. Some to measles, some to smallpox, some to other illnesses. I had cried myself to sleep hundreds of nights.

I thought the whole world was like that. I didn't know until I came to America that my friends had not needed to die. I was amazed at all the medicine that was available in America. I was appalled when I saw the grocery stores and all the food. And for a while I was angry because so many children were dying in poor nations and so few people in America seemed to care. But over time I realized the problem was not how few people cared but how few people even knew.

I wish I could tell you that the drums no longer beat in that village. I wish I could report that poverty has been eradicated, that precious little children no longer die needlessly. But you know as well as I do that the world is even more unstable, more dangerous, more impoverished, and more in need of a Savior than it was during my own childhood.

God Himself warned us that poverty would not simply go away. As Deuteronomy 15:11 says, "There will always be poor people in the land." But God did not say that so we would despair or shrug our shoulders, but so we would open our eyes to the needs of the poor and respond with generosity and compassion. Too often we forget the second half of the verse: "Therefore I command you to be openhanded toward your brothers and toward the poor and needy in your land."

This command is not unique in Scripture. The Law of Moses, the Psalms, the Proverbs, the Prophets, the Gospels, and the Epistles all teach that caring for the poor is part of loving and honoring God. One of my favorite examples is found in the book of Isaiah: "If you do away with the yoke of oppression, with the pointing finger and malicious talk, and if you spend yourselves in behalf of the hungry and satisfy the needs of the oppressed, then your light will rise in the darkness, and your night will become like the noonday" (Isaiah 58:9b–10).

I am intrigued by the prophet's challenge: "Spend yourselves in behalf of the hungry." Could it be that God wants us to invest not just our money but also our time, our hearts, our very selves? Could it be that God wants to break our hearts for the little ones who are dying of hunger, to give us compassion for the young people who have lost all hope?

And then there's the call to "satisfy the needs of the oppressed." It takes commitment and personal involvement to satisfy the needs of impoverished children. Children's needs, after all, are not just economic but also physical, social, and spiritual. They need to maintain good health, to learn how to read, to acquire life skills, and to understand God's Word. They need to know their Savior and to know that people love them and want them to succeed.

Over the last 50 years, Compassion has partnered with local churches to satisfy the needs of nearly a million precious children. Yet there are millions and millions more whom we cannot reach without your help. We invite you—we *urge* you—to invest your time, your heart, yourself on behalf of these children.

Begin by simply reading this book. In the pages that follow you'll encounter stories of real children in the circumstances that threaten them daily. You'll learn more about their needs and about the ways to meet them. Please provide others that same opportunity by making this book available to them. Share it with your friends and family so that more of us can begin to know and care about the needs of children living in poverty.

One is about God's people coming together with one heart, one mind, and one spirit to fulfill our calling to the poor. *One* is about you answering God's call to reach out in Jesus' name to His little ones. *One* is about all of us knowing, caring, and responding with compassion.

ALL FOR THE CAUSE OF CHRIST
ALL FOR THE GLORY OF GOD
ALL FOR THE MILLIONS OF CHILDREN
WAITING TO BE RELEASED FROM POVERTY
IN JESUS' NAME

com·pas·sion, *n.* deep sympathy for the suffering of another, accompanied by the desire to relieve it.

one

Compassion's story is the story of *One*. It began in the heart of one man: Compassion's founder, Everett Swanson. It reaches one world—the world God has entrusted to us—filled with His children in need. It forges one resolve: to establish and enhance a ministry to children in need that will touch every area of their lives. That ministry is focused on one child at a time because every child has his or her own dreams, joys, and needs.

Caring Christians have taken on the unique role of sponsor to the children we serve—one sponsor linked to one child. Over the years, many Christians have joined together behind one cause: the cause of reaching children in Jesus' name. Because of them, we have 50 years of vital ministry to celebrate.

And the story of *One* will continue, because we are dedicated to meeting one challenge together. We are determined to reach across oceans—and across our towns—to help each child of poverty fulfill his or her God-given potential.

You are an important part of our story, because we cannot meet the challenge without your help. We urge you to serve the needy ones God has placed within your reach. Together—as one—we can do much in Jesus' name for the children He loved enough to die for.

one man

HONG KONG

Compassion
7774 Irving Park Road
Chicago, Illinois 60634

IMPORTANT

SPONSORSHIP PAPERS ENCLOSED

FOR #93 Good Neighbor – #393 Koo Yung Mo

SPONSORED BY Mr. and Mrs. Robert A. Stroup

PLEASE KEEP WITH VALUABLE PAPERS

No. 440 — Wan Jin

REV. EVERETT SWANSON went to Korea because he was offered the opportunity to preach to thousands of military personnel engaged in the Korean conflict. Here, Swanson addresses South Korean troops with a message of hope—the same hope that would soon lead him to reach out to Korea's children. *Archive photo.*

"I HAVE COMPASSION ON THE
MULTITUDE . . . I WILL NOT
SEND THEM AWAY. . . ."

Matthew 15:32, KJV

One morning half a century ago, a preacher took an early morning walk through the streets of Seoul, South Korea.

Everett Swanson was an American evangelist from the Swedish Baptist denomination. For years he had preached the gospel with passion and urgency in the United States. When the invitation came for him to conduct services for thousands of troops in Japan and Korea, Everett eagerly took the opportunity.

The 1952 Korean preaching tour was an unqualified success. Hundreds of souls had been won to the Kingdom of God. Everett could leave the country in a few days satisfied that his mission had been accomplished and accomplished well.

The city of Seoul was just beginning to stir that day. The brisk morning air was having an effect on Everett. He was waking up—and remembering.

Everett Swanson couldn't escape the images of the war orphans he'd seen. There were so many. They might escape the cross fire of local skirmishes, but they could never escape the cultural disgrace of being orphans.

And then there were the scores of children he'd held who had been abandoned. Having a Korean mother and an American father isolated them as few other circumstances could.

The country didn't seem to know what to do with these victims of war. Everett didn't either. Try as he might to change his train of thought that morning, he couldn't shake the faces of the innocents he'd encountered.

The chug of a flatbed truck shook him out of his reverie. He glanced up as the truck came to a halt a few blocks ahead of him. Workers poured from the cab to gather what appeared to be a few piles of rags from doorways and alleys down the street. They threw the rags onto the truck bed.

6

EVERETT SWANSON encountered the face of poverty
where he least expected it: Korean street children
like this. *Archive photo.*

Everett continued on his walk. As he drew closer to the truck, he noticed the workers gently kicking the rag piles as they came across them. That made sense; rats were common.

One rag pile lay in a doorway not far from Everett. He was set to reach it at about the same time as one of the workers.

That's when Everett noticed that the pile had more than rags in it. A small arm extended from the pile, and Everett began to make out the shape of a child sleeping in a fetal position under the rags. He ran to warn the worker not to kick those rags.

But somehow, as he ran, Everett caught sight of the cargo on the flatbed truck. He stopped cold in his tracks as he realized what he was witnessing.

The workers' mission had never been to gather rags. It had been to gather the bodies of abandoned children who had died on the streets overnight. Some of these children had begged Everett for spare change in the few days just passed.

Some of the abandoned children, like the boy Everett had noticed in the doorway, would wake to face another day. Being kicked by a city sanitation worker was as normal a wake-up call for those children as a mother's voice and the smell of bacon and eggs were for the children Everett encountered in churches throughout the United States.

7

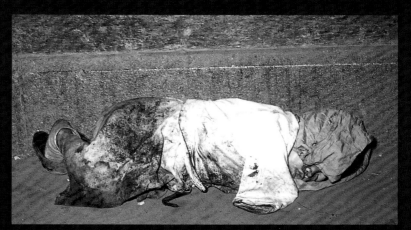

KOREAN STREET children in the early 1950s often made the sidewalks their beds. From a distance, a child could look like a pile of rags—much the same way this sleeping child looked through Everett Swanson's camera lens. *Archive photo.*

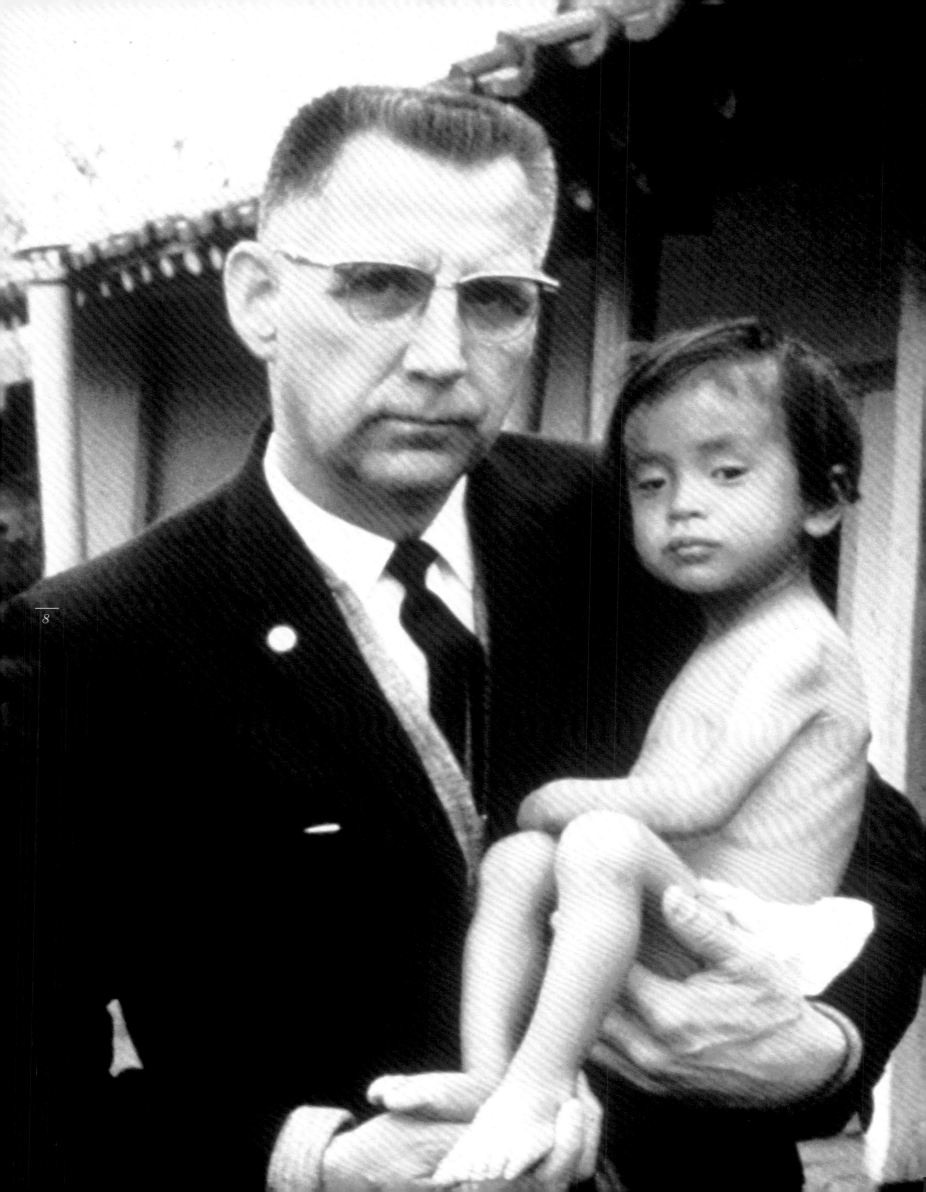

(Above) **SWANSON'S PREACHING** services during the Korean conflict often took place in tents belonging to mobile military units. *Archive photo.*

(Left) Early on, Everett Swanson recognized the importance of giving individual attention to the neglected children he met on the streets of Korea. *Archive photo.*

And Everett Swanson had seen no one stepping forward on behalf of the children.

Everett's head was still swimming, and his heart was troubled, when he met with a missionary friend in Korea. He recounted the details of his preaching tour to his friend. He reviewed the successes there. Yet the conversation constantly drifted back to Korea's children, to the social stigma of the orphans and mixed-race children, to the bitterness of the poverty they suffered.

His missionary friend offered no easy answers. Instead, he simply said, "You have seen the tremendous needs and unparalleled opportunities of this land. What do you intend to do about it?"

Everett Swanson took that challenge to heart. He would say later that the propellers on the plane which carried him back across the Pacific to the United States kept humming, *What do you intend to do about it? What do you intend to do about it?* With the question confronting him throughout the flight, Everett determined to do something for the needy Korean children he'd seen. He wasn't sure what form his assistance would take. Nor had he any idea where he would get financial backing.

(Above) **COMPASSION'S WORK** began with one orphanage. Over time, Compassion was able to celebrate the construction of facilities, like this one, that could provide shelter and care for many more children in need. *Archive photo.*

(Left) One of Swanson's special joys was distributing warm clothing to protect the orphans from the bitterly cold Korean winters. *Archive photo.*

But he didn't have to wait long to find out. The day his plane landed in Seattle, someone gave him $50 designated "for Korea." When he arrived at his Chicago home, a $1,000 check earmarked "for the needy of Korea" was waiting for him. Everett would later write, "This was conclusive proof to me that God was in it."

Everett first used his evangelistic platform in the United States to raise money to support an orphanage in Korea. Later, as Korean Christians began new orphanages—some by converting their own homes into dormitories—Everett also raised funds to support their work.

Yet there was a need for ongoing support for the children and for a way to make each child's progress important. So Everett developed a one-to-one sponsorship program. The program allowed an individual in the United States to provide Bible-based education, food, clothing, shelter, and medical care for an at-risk Korean child—and all for just a few dollars a month.

에버레트 에후 스완슨 목사

이 분은 우리 고아 백삼십팔명으로 하여금
하나님의 사랑 속에서 자라날수 있도록 보호자를
맺어주신 그신 은혜와 근심양면으로 도와 주심에
감사하여 어린이들 스스로 이 분을 복음의사자로
하나님의 은총과 함께 그 공훈한 뜻을 오래오래
찬양 하고져 이 비를 세움.
단기4293년 3월13일

REV. EVERETT F. SWANSON
WE ERECT THIS MONUMENT IN HONOR OF
DR. SWANSON WHO HAS HELPED ONE HUNDRED
AND THIRTY-EIGHT ORPHANS BOTH SPIRITUALLY
AND MATERIALLY TO BRING THEM UP IN THE MERCY
OF GOD. WE PRAISE HIS CHARITABLE DEEDS AND
CONTRIBUTIONS FOR THE ORPHANS AND THE GRACIOUS
WILL OF OUR LORD JESUS CHRIST FOR EVER."
MARCH 13, 1960

(Above) **EVERETT AND** Miriam Swanson set a precedent that almost every Compassion staff member has followed since: they were Compassion sponsors. Here, the Swansons hold two of their sponsored children. *Archive photo.*

(Left) This plaque is one of many expressions of gratitude given to Everett Swanson in Korea in response to his dedication to the children. *Archive photo.*

The sponsorship program was a way that an ordinary family could afford to support a child in need. Ten years after Everett dealt with the question posed by his missionary friend, more than 10,000 Korean children were sponsored. The volume of children being served demanded a move of the ministry headquarters from Everett's basement to an office building on Irving Park Road in Chicago. And soon after, the Everett Swanson Evangelistic Association changed its name to Compassion Incorporated.

The name came from Matthew 15:32, the verse that had appeared at the top of Everett's newsletter for many years: "I have compassion on the multitude . . . I will not send them away. . ."(KJV).

This verse was a promise that changed the lives of thousands of Korean children who would otherwise have been abandoned. In fact, it is a promise that still changes lives today. It is a promise that holds true because, half a century ago, one man had compassion on children in need. And instead of running from them, he embraced them.

So we follow Everett Swanson's example, as he followed the example of Jesus. Embracing children in need is the heart of Compassion.

one world

"LORD, WHEN DID WE SEE YOU HUNGRY AND FEED YOU, OR THIRSTY AND GIVE YOU SOMETHING TO DRINK? WHEN DID WE SEE YOU A STRANGER AND INVITE YOU IN, OR NEEDING CLOTHES AND CLOTHE YOU? WHEN DID WE SEE YOU SICK OR IN PRISON AND GO TO VISIT YOU?"

Matthew 25:37–39

There are times when poverty hides. You don't always notice a child's problems when you first meet him or her. More often, you're charmed by a smile or captivated by a positive attitude in the most difficult of surroundings. Some serious afflictions—malnutrition, disease, even abuse—may not visibly affect a child for some time.

There are other times when poverty screams. Children caught in violence, children used as warm bodies in a sweatshop or a brothel, children sniffing glue to keep hunger pains under control—these are all situations that don't need analysis. Instead, all over the world, they need answers.

When Everett Swanson's eyes were opened to the needs of children in Korea, he quickly learned to look for the poverty that is hidden behind a smile as well as the poverty that loudly demands intervention. He set a precedent for Compassion to look beneath the surface for the long-term needs of the children we serve—and to see our service to them as ministry to the Lord Himself.

(Above) **IN MANY SLUMS**, the majority of the inhabitants are children. This run-down neighborhood in Bangalore, India, is no exception.

(Right) A young Rwandan refugee huddles close to his mother. His mother is clutching a ticket that can be exchanged for food rations at a refugee repatriation center.

TWO BOYS dive into the Nan River in Phitsanulok, Thailand. Seasonal rains often wash away the homes, which in the dry season sit high on the river's banks.

YOSIMAR MATHEU helps at home by caring for his little brother while his parents work.

the poverty curve

The last two decades have brought an amazing economic growth curve to developed countries. We live in a day of instant information and easy access to food, medicine, and entertainment.

Of course, that easy access depends on where you live. At the same time the economy was going through the roof for many of us, the number of people living in poverty grew to 1.2 billion. That's one in every five of us living on the planet. And 600 million of those in poverty are children.[1]

When poverty strikes, it is often the children who are most affected. Adults get sick when a disease sweeps through a shantytown; children often die. Adults lose weight in a time of drought; children often starve. Adults plan the machinations of war and political violence; children get caught in the cross fire.

How long will we allow poverty to rob us of the world's children?

malnutrition

The good news is, the mortality rate for children dying from malnutrition and preventable diseases has dropped significantly over the past 20 years.

The bad news is that 10 million children under the age of five still die every year,[2] and more than half of these deaths are associated with malnutrition.[3] Irreversible blindness still strikes about 250,000 children each year due to a simple lack of vitamin A.[4] And 33 percent of young children in developing countries still suffer from stunted growth, physically or mentally, because of inadequate nourishment.[5]

To end this travesty, the proper foods—and enough of them—must be available to children. Frequently, the children Compassion serves come to us with full bellies but an unbalanced diet. They will suffer the effects of malnutrition unless they receive intervention.

It looks like the old saying is true: You are what you eat. And too many children still go without adequate nutrition.

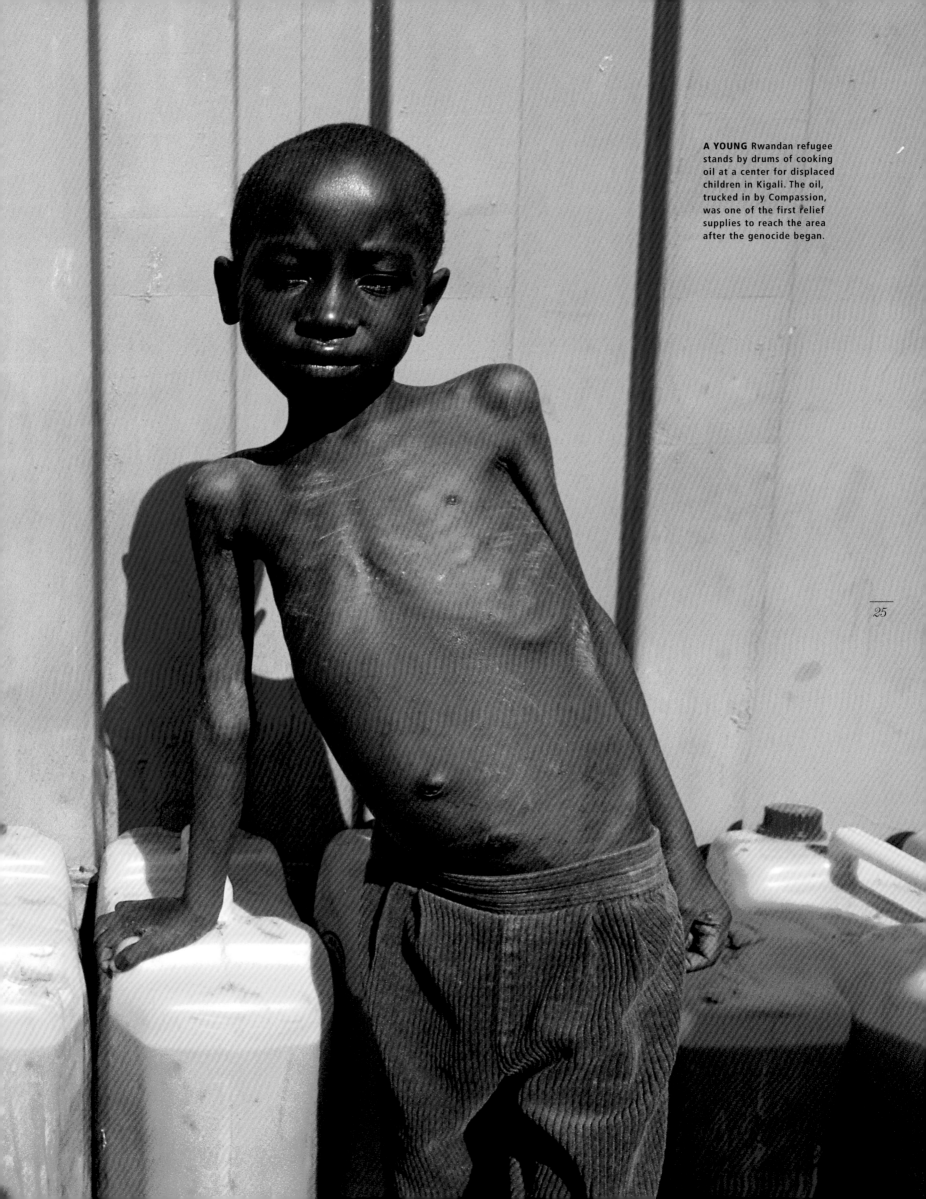

25

SCORES OF children, with their daily food ration of a bowl of porridge, fill a refugee camp in Africa.

illiteracy

Learning to read opens up horizons of knowledge. And when knowledge is applied, it becomes empowerment. Perhaps that is why experts regularly identify literacy as one of the most important factors in overcoming poverty.

Yet more than 130 million elementary-school-aged children in developing countries do not attend school.[6] Many were taken out of school to supplement family incomes by working. Others live in countries where conflict or natural disasters have forced the suspension of school. Even when school is in session, fees and tuition payments can keep a child's education well out of reach for poor families.

Nearly 60 percent of children who are not in school are girls, many of them denied the opportunity for education because of their gender.[7] Some cultures find it unseemly to have boys and girls in the same classroom. If separate facilities are not available, male students alone go to school. In other societies, the traditional roles of homemaker and mother are not valued enough to demand even a basic education for girls.

When the horizons of knowledge are denied to a child, the child's potential is denied to the world. All of us miss out on the talents and abilities that child could bring to mankind.

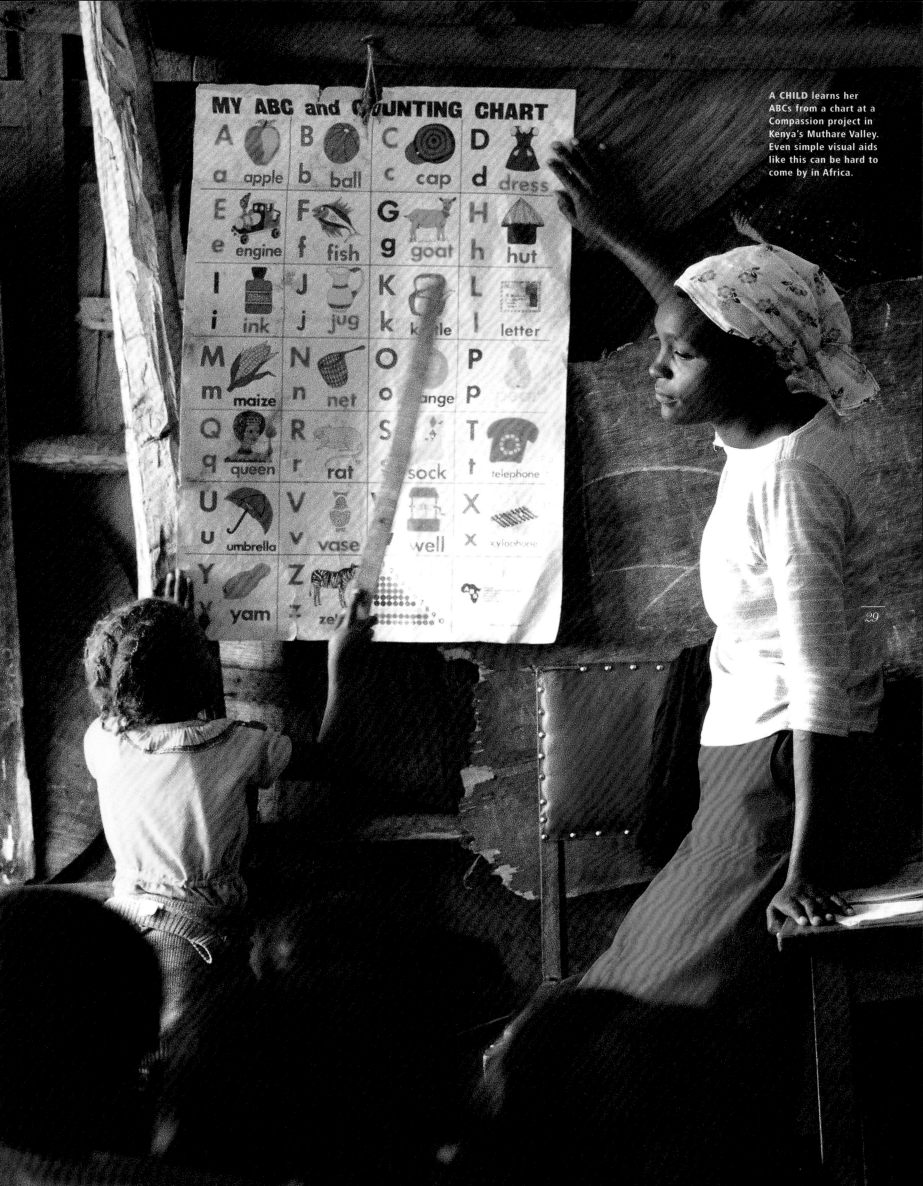

A CHILD learns her ABCs from a chart at a Compassion project in Kenya's Muthare Valley. Even simple visual aids like this can be hard to come by in Africa.

29

MIGUEL ANGEL TUBAY reads a book that he received from his Compassion project in Ecuador.

31

disease

For the poor, diseases like mumps and measles are still killers. Although great progress has been made in child immunization, more than one-fourth of children in developing countries still go without the vaccinations that could save their lives. For example, only 74 percent of one-year-olds in developing countries have been fully immunized for polio, and only 70 percent have been immunized for measles.[8]

The last decade has witnessed the onslaught of another, more insidious killer. When Compassion staff were first introduced to AIDS in some of the East African communities we serve, the locals called it "the robber." As we became more aware of the impact AIDS has on families and children, we found no better name for it. AIDS has taken out young adults with brutality and speed, leaving children without parents, aunts, and uncles. An alarming number of children have been left as heads of households.

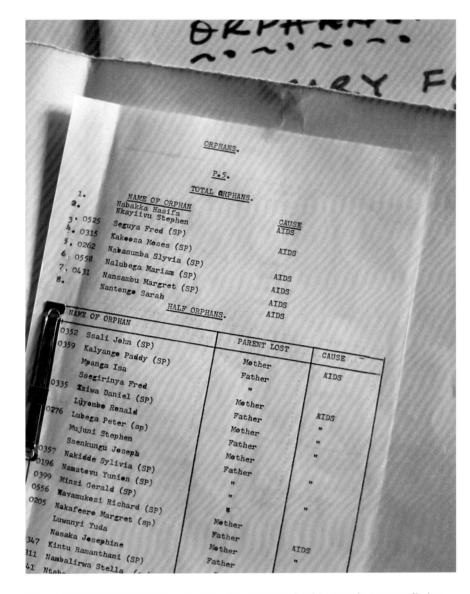

(Above) **AT THE COMPASSION**-assisted Masaka Baptist School in Uganda, a roster listing orphans—and their parents' causes of death—reveals the alarming pace of AIDS in sub-Saharan Africa.

(Left) Children with AIDS, like this one, fill up many of the beds at Kitovu Hospital in Masaka, Uganda. This hospital serves an area in southern Uganda hit hard by the AIDS pandemic.

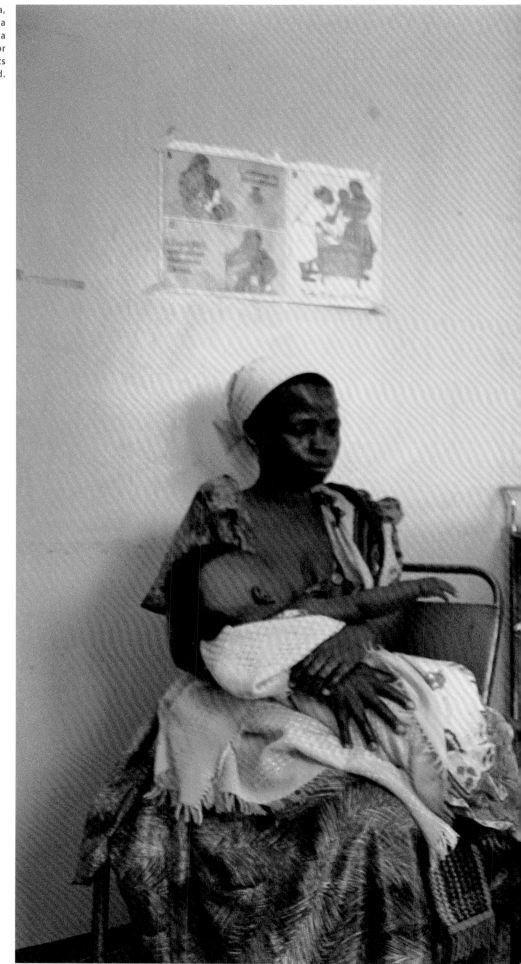

AT A HOSPITAL in Masaka, Uganda, Sister Monica Prendergast prepares a 10-month-old boy for burial while a mother waits for her child to be treated.

African AIDS victims in the last decade greatly outnumbered the victims of more publicized armed conflicts. In 1998 alone, 2 million Africans died from AIDS[9]—more than six times the number of people killed in the Bosnian conflict.[10]

HIV/AIDS is also reaching crisis proportions in other places where Compassion works, and it doesn't spare the children. Every day, 8,500 children and young people around the world become infected with HIV.[11] That's a rate of over 3 million children a year.

"The robber" won't be leaving us anytime soon.

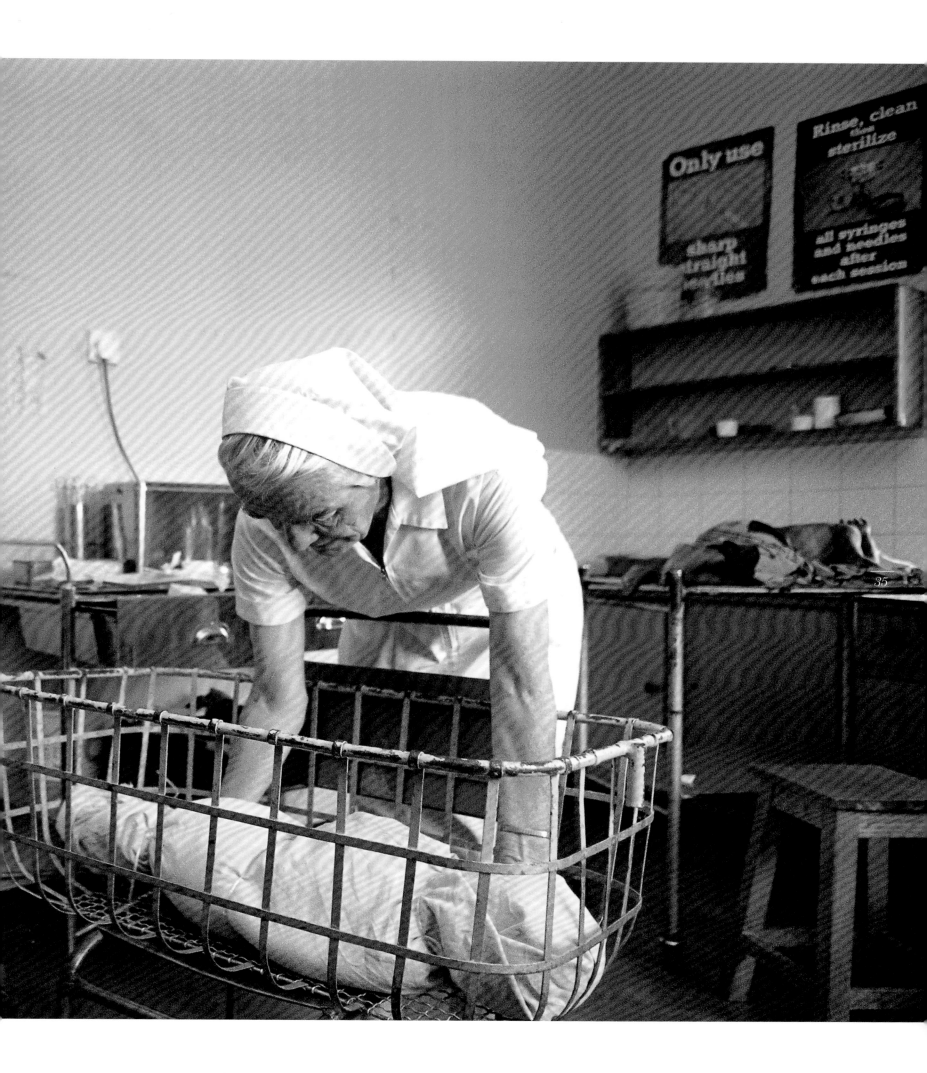

36

(Right) **A GIRL** works in the rice fields of Nepal.

(Left) A school-age girl carries sand at a construction site in Bangalore, India. Many girls in developing countries are required to join the work force at an early age.

39

child labor

It's nearly universally agreed upon: making a living is to be put off until a child has received an education. And children are never to be put at risk to earn a dollar.

Such ideals might cause one to think that child labor is no longer an issue. But for 250 million children between 5 and 14 years old who live in developing countries, making a living any way they can is still a reality.[12] Many of these children had to leave school—or missed the opportunity for schooling completely—in order to supplement a meager family income.

An estimated 50 to 60 million children between the ages of 5 and 11 work in hazardous situations.[13] More than 300,000 children, many under the age of 10, are serving as soldiers.[14] There's no way to count the number of children exploited by forced recruitment into drug trafficking, prostitution, or pornography. It is hard to estimate how many others were sold into a life of labor to settle a debt or to provide quick cash for a desperately needy family.[15]

No matter where a child lives, or how destitute his or her family may be, every child deserves a childhood.

YOUNG BOYS haul heavy loads of reeds from fields near their homes in Guatemala. The reeds will be woven into mats or used for construction.

(Right) **SHADOWS OF** neighbors darken the wall of a Kigali, Rwanda, neighborhood. This is the site of a massacre where a family of seven—four of them children—were forced into a hole in the ground and killed with hand grenades. The hole became the family's tomb. It was sealed over by neighbors, and the date of the massacre was inscribed in the concrete cover.

(Left) A 12-year-old girl, her face still healing from a machete blow, sips milk porridge supplied by Compassion. The girl survived the Rwandan carnage by pretending to be dead.

war

Politically motivated violence is often a single step away from bedlam.

In the last decade, the world watched in astonishment as local militias butchered entire neighborhoods and villages in areas as diverse as Rwanda, Yugoslavia, and East Timor. When regional politics became armed violence in Haiti, the Democratic Republic of Congo, and the Mexican state of Chiapas, children often became the first victims.

Life loses every sense of normalcy for a child in a war zone. School is usually suspended. Food supplies become unstable. Families are often scattered.

Ninety percent of war's victims are civilian—and most are women and children.[16] In the last decade of the 20th century, more than 2 million children were killed in armed conflicts. Another 6 million were injured or disabled. Tens of thousands became victims of land mines. Those are the physical statistics of war.[17]

But just as disturbing is the emotional and psychological impact on a child who witnesses extreme violence at close range. Shortly after the Rwandan genocide of 1994, a staff member at a Compassion student center commented, "The children don't sing anymore. They saw too many adults killing their neighbors and families. They don't know whom to trust. We have a generation facing us who may never again believe anything we tell them."

When children live in a situation just one step away from bedlam, is it any wonder they don't trust?

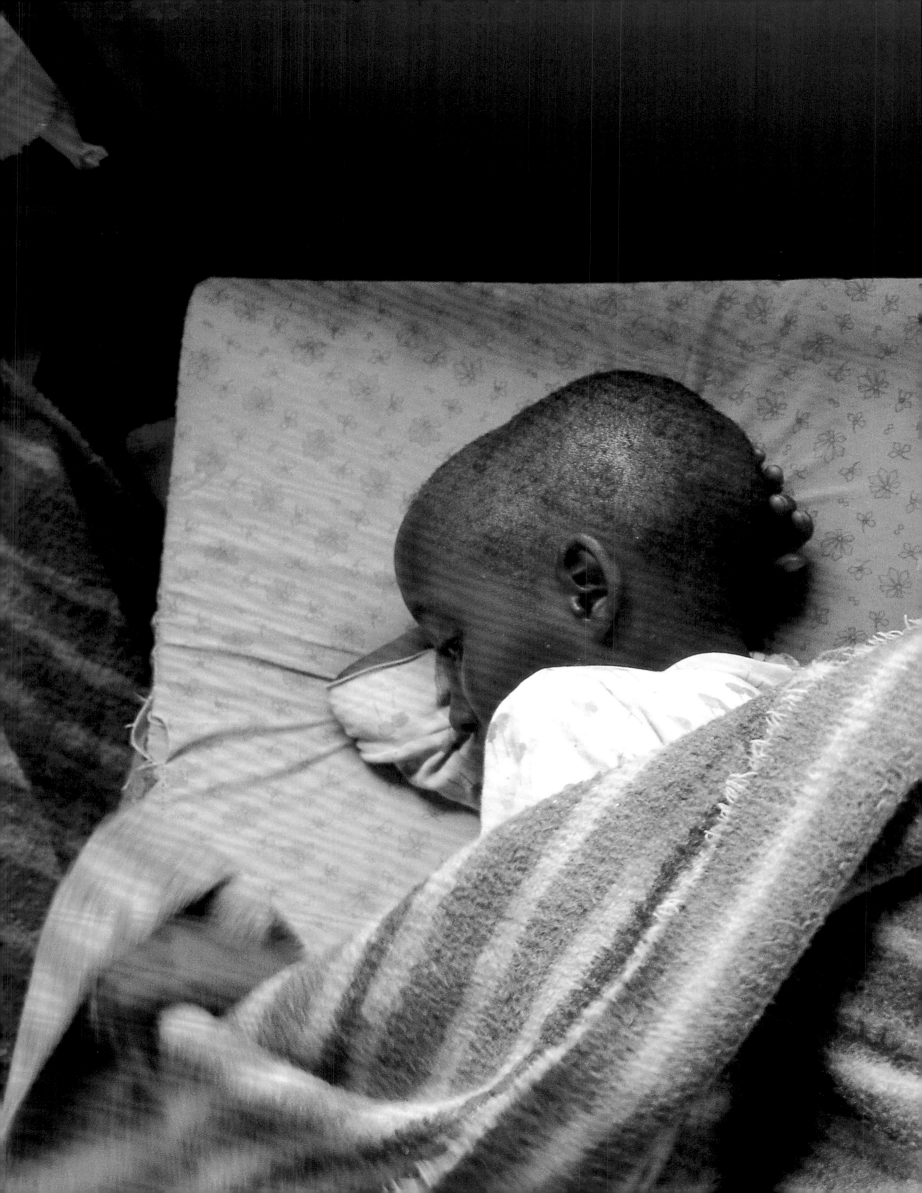

TWO YOUNG boys orphaned in the Rwandan genocide share a bed in a Compassion-assisted orphanage in Kigali. In the months following the violence, this facility was packed with children. Often two or three children shared a single bed.

A DISCARDED tire in a slum of Mexico City provides a boy with shelter.

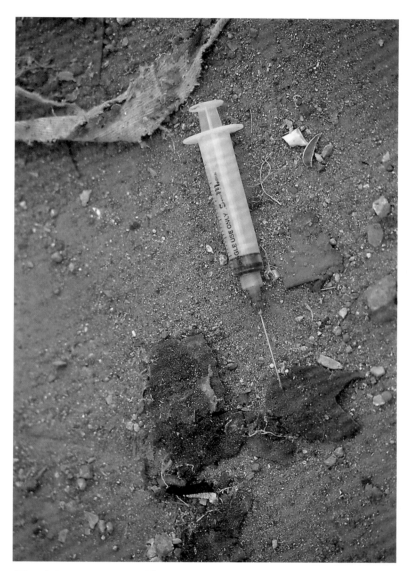

(Above) **ON THE WAY** to and from Compassion projects, children often have to walk through neighborhoods littered with drug paraphernalia.

(Left) A homeless boy warms himself by a street fire in Katmandu, Nepal.

one resolve

Proverbs 22:6

Compassion's response to a world in need is based on a simple resolve: to develop children into all God intended them to be.

This is not a platitude. It's a strategy we've followed for 50 years. It calls us to offer children the opportunity to grow in every area of life. It demands that we do what is necessary to develop them into whole, fulfilled Christian adults—just as our mission statement says.

So how does Compassion bring wholeness and development to the children in our program?

Training in God's Word is one key. It not only affirms the value of children but also leads many to a relationship with Jesus Christ. Formal education opens up a world of opportunities and information to children surrounded by poverty. Nonformal education, which often involves vocational training, prepares those children to meet the challenges of life in their environment. Teaching the children basic hygiene has proven to be a huge deterrent against disease. The simple skill of getting along with others is vital in building citizenship. Since Christian teaching, education, health, and social skills should all be part of children's lives, they are all a part of our program.

Our single resolve—to develop children into all God intended them to be—is not some romantic reaction to the challenges poverty puts in a child's path. Rather, it places God's wisdom at the heart of what we do. It recognizes His handiwork in every child we serve.

It also points each child to a future secured in the ways and Word of God.

SHARING IS a necessary social skill. It's also an everyday reality at this student center in Chennai, India, where children double up to make textbooks and other learning materials go farther.

SPONSORED CHILDREN around the world take the power of prayer seriously. These children at the Jeevauhalli Student Center in Bangalore, India, take a few moments to pause before the Lord.

Christian training: child disciples in the works

Every child is created, known, and loved by God. Compassion believes that every child, then, deserves to know the Heavenly Father.

Across cultures and languages, Compassion brings the gospel to the children we serve. Of the many things we do, giving children the opportunity to learn about Jesus Christ is the most important.

That's why we take care to present the gospel consistently. This can happen through Bible studies at an after-school program, during daily devotional times in a church-related school, or as part of a church's regular Christian education program.

COMPASSION IS committed to supplying every registered child in our program with a Bible he or she can understand. God's written word is a welcome gift to this Indonesian boy at a Bandung project.

Compassion makes the gospel plain to the children by both word and deed. The children hear about Jesus through age-appropriate, culturally relevant lessons. They also see the gospel in action by the way staff members and teachers treat them.

Children must be allowed to choose a relationship with Jesus Christ and to grow in that relationship as individuals. We can't coerce any child into a relationship with God. Nor can we expect every child to pursue discipleship at the same pace.

But Compassion does have the responsibility to provide opportunities for a child to develop in the ways and Word of God. Our goal for the children we serve is wholeness—and that includes spiritual wholeness. That means giving them the opportunities to participate in prayer and Bible study. Compassion helps the children work through everyday issues, ranging from relationships with friends and family to work ethics and sexual purity, with God's Word as their guide.

We believe that the most important thing we can do is to introduce a child to the Savior who bids every child to come to Him. We've seen it work time and again: once a child truly understands the depth of God's love, he or she tends to flourish in every other area of life.

The whole gospel for the whole child is the basis of a fulfilled life—both today and for eternity.

SIRIPORN KASAEJITSOMPOP reads from the Bible in the doorway of her rural home near Chiongdao, Thailand. Often Compassion-supplied Bibles are the only reading material in a home.

SPONSORS AND staff often remark that sponsored children seem very enthusiastic about learning. These children are no exception as they race to class at a project near Meru, Kenya.

62

ROSEMARY
NABAKOOZA
demonstrates her
perfect penmanship.
Despite losing her
arms to a wild boar,
she has learned to
read and write with
the help of the
Nakatete Child
Development Center
in southern Uganda.

LEADERSHIP SKILLS are encouraged in Compassion's child development program. Here, a young lady leads her class in speech exercises in Chennai, India.

formal education: literacy and more

Early in Compassion's ministry, it was not uncommon to hear frustration in a staff member's voice about government pamphlets being distributed in the areas we served. The problem usually wasn't the content. It was simply that so few people had the ability to read.

A farmer could have a piece of paper with words on it that could increase his crop yield by 50 percent. A day laborer could have a brochure that explained the dangers of pirating electricity from a transformer. A citizen could have information on the date and time of the next election. And in every case, the people holding the papers were unable to act on the information because they couldn't read.

Literacy for every child we serve soon became a driving passion for Compassion's child development program. It gave rise to an emphasis on formal education—the classroom experience that would make a child proficient in reading, writing, and arithmetic.

These skills change a child's life. They also open up a vast horizon of information that could bring a positive revolution to an impoverished family. For years, we have seen sponsored children learn how to read and then teach parents or siblings the same skill.

The results can be dramatic. Parents can gain better employment simply because they can read and write. Children gain a new sense of worth and an expanded notion of their future options.

It's a tried-and-true principle: The most basic education can change a child's life.

You're reading this page, aren't you?

nonformal education: skills for life

Many of the children we serve come to us with well-developed street smarts. They've learned how to survive in some of the most difficult environments imaginable.

Nonformal education is how Compassion gives "life smarts" to these children. This part of Compassion's program brings children the kind of hands-on experience that can change their lives in the future—and right now.

Sometimes this means giving children the opportunity to visit parts of their countries that they might otherwise never see—museums, libraries, and nature reserves. It can mean time at a camp that allows them to experience teamwork and see more of God's creation.

HYDROPONICS MIGHT help this boy at the Maranatha Student Center in Lima, Peru, to someday provide food for his family.

65

COMPASSION'S NONFORMAL Education Fund supplements sponsorship dollars to train children in practical, marketable skills. Sewing, farming, and carpentry are featured in the vocational training here at the Mulu Wongel Student Center in Holeta, Ethiopia.

ONE GOAL of Compassion's child development program is for children to contribute to the local economy when they become adults. The practical skills these girls in Bangalore, India, are learning will make them employable when they complete their formal education.

More often, nonformal education teaches children skills that could help stabilize their economic situation. The skills a Compassion project offers are based on the needs of the local marketplace. That means a child in rural Uganda might learn animal husbandry and how to make bricks. In a growing Brazilian city, young men about to enter the work force might learn carpentry. Over time, these skills combine with formal education to produce children far better prepared to meet the challenges of life than the generations who came before them.

Every skill taught in Compassion's nonformal education program adds to a child's foundation of "life smarts." Just as important, every skill shows children that they can be contributors to their environment, not victims of it.

68

TRAINING CHILDREN in basic hygiene and healthcare practices is crucial to improving their well-being. For these children in Boqueraio de Cesaria, Brazil, even brushing their teeth after a midday snack is a learning experience.

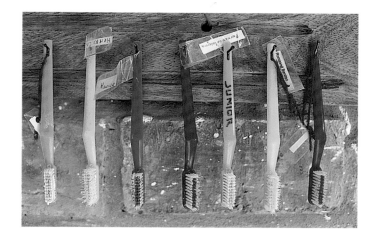

BRUSHES TAGGED with students' names hang on a project wall in Cochabamba, Bolivia.

healthcare:
intervention and training

Early in Compassion's history, healthcare meant making food available to children. Later, vaccinations prevented trouble from diseases like measles and diphtheria.

These initial steps established Compassion's pattern of correcting children's existing health problems and curtailing future threats to their well-being. Stabilizing a child's diet is still crucial in this strategy, as are vaccinations. But so is teaching a child basic hygiene. Washing your hands properly and knowing how to brush your teeth are just as important to preventing disease as vaccinations are. Knowing how to monitor your own health, and how to help those around you monitor theirs, can bring intervention in the early stages of a disease and often prevent it from becoming life threatening.

For example, Compassion teaches children how to recognize the warning signs of dehydration. We also teach children and their parents how to administer oral rehydration therapy to those suffering from disease-related dehydration. It's a simple process that saves lives.

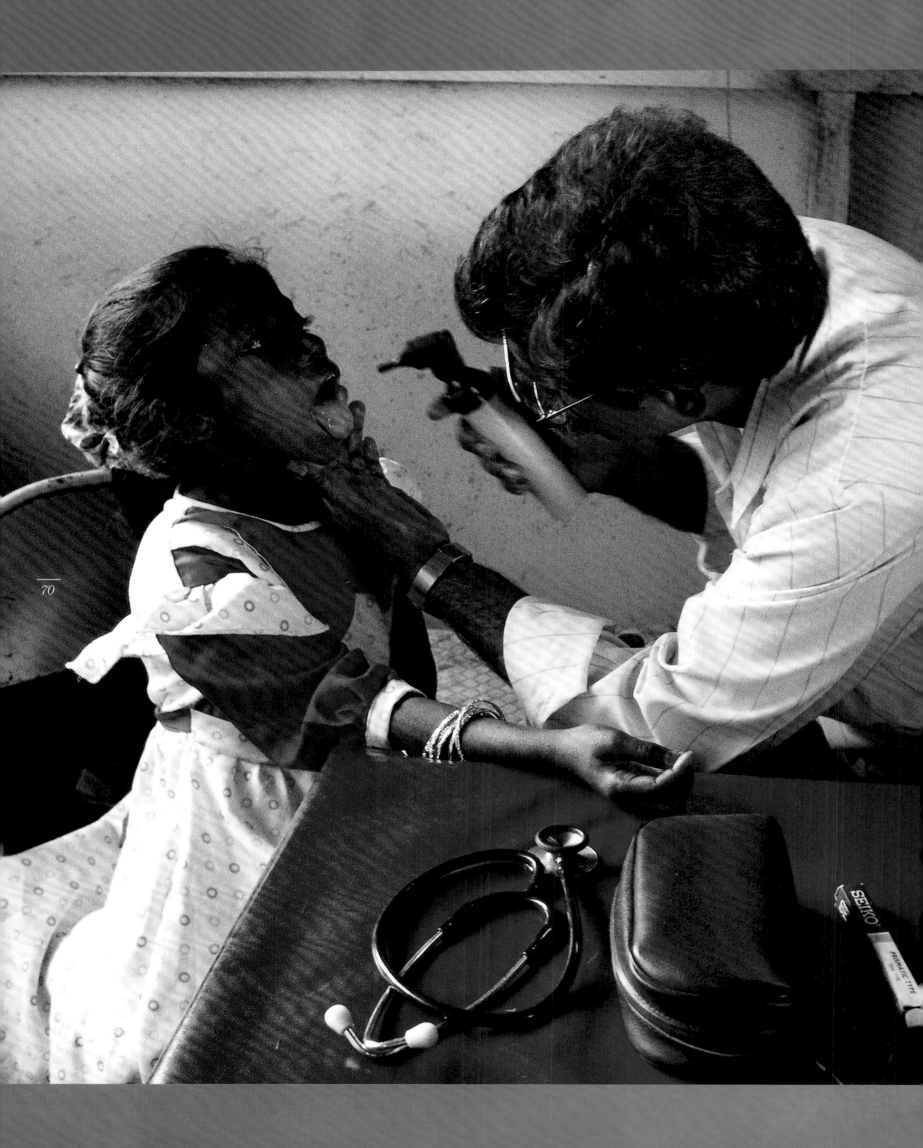

THE CHILDREN Compassion serves often go home to challenging conditions. Here, a government health worker fills out a report on unclean drinking water found at a home in Peten, Guatemala, not far from a student center. The water contained live mosquito larvae and other parasites.

71

Not all problems have simple or inexpensive solutions. The generosity of sponsors and donors allows Compassion to take extraordinary measures for children who need extended treatment for burns, disabilities, heart abnormalities, and common injuries such as broken arms.

In recent years, children have come face-to-face with the devastation of AIDS. Thousands of the children we serve have lost one or both parents to AIDS. Hundreds more are HIV-positive themselves. In the face of the new challenges presented by this pandemic, Compassion is bringing the training and intervention needed to help these children live as best they can.

You may not have *everything* if you have your health. But for the children we serve, health is one key to overcoming poverty.

LUNCH AT a student center is sometimes the only hot food a child receives that day.

nutrition: food for thought and growth

It's no surprise that proper nutrition makes a huge difference in the lives of poverty-stricken children. From our beginning, Compassion understood that a hungry child would focus on little else but food until his or her stomach was filled.

But a full stomach isn't enough. In rural areas where seasonal fruit is plentiful and nearly free for the taking, children can suffer from malnutrition even though they don't have hunger pangs. They eat their fill of fruit, and their hunger is silenced. But that means their families sometimes ignore their need for fats and proteins. And in the city, market prices often dictate the food selection (or lack of it) on the tables of impoverished families. In either case, it takes only a few weeks for the effects of malnutrition to begin to show in a child.

Compassion teaches both children and their families the significance of a balanced diet at home. We instruct them in how to bring a balanced diet to their tables from local and affordable resources. Many Compassion projects also offer a balanced selection of snacks or meals to sponsored children and sometimes provide additional food to families in special need.

Does it make a difference? The children we serve are in some of the most active years of development. Without adequate nutrition, their physical and mental growth will be stunted. With proper nutrition, they can develop normally. Children can focus on their schoolwork better and gain the physical reserves they need to combat illness and infections.

Good nutrition truly provides both food for the body and food for thought. Perhaps that's why Jesus made feeding the hungry a part of His ministry to the whole person.

MEALS AND snacks served at Compassion student centers—like this one in Nairobi, Kenya—are designed to balance out children's diets.

COOKS STIR large pots of maize porridge at a student center in Arusha, Tanzania. The porridge is served as a snack to the students.

Poverty strips stability away from communities, families, and children alike. Community standards for behavior can easily deteriorate when simple necessities—food, sanitation, drinking water, fuel—are inaccessible. Many of the children Compassion serves are exposed daily to a survival-of–the-fittest mentality in their neighborhood that expresses itself through theft or violence.

Families can fragment under the pressure of poverty. Fathers and mothers sometimes must choose between roles as breadwinners and caregivers—often, the resources aren't available to do both. The despair that comes with poverty can easily drive some adults into abusing drugs, alcohol, and even other family members.

The children we serve often live with the constant stress and confusion of shifting roles: caregiver to younger siblings, contributor to the family income, and growing child still learning how to deal with everyday life.

What forces combine to shape children? The communities and families that surround them certainly play a big role. And when the forces of poverty bring chaos to a child's world, Compassion offers opportunities for that child to build healthy relationships and learn respect for others. Safe and supervised recreation, team-building activities, group learning in and out of the classroom, even learning how to line up—all make a difference in helping a child find order in life and a place in the world.

CHILDREN AT the Christian Mission Student Center in Chennai, India, practice forming a line.

STUDENTS LIKE this one in Chiang Rai, Thailand, are anxious to share their newfound knowledge in class.

CHILDREN PLAY a group game at a project near Nairobi, Kenya.

78

local church partnerships:
the delivery system

Thousands of Compassion sponsors have visited our local projects over the years. Many of them have expressed surprise that Compassion often isn't mentioned in the sign that lets the neighborhood know the project is there.

That's because our local partners are local churches. We want our partners' neighbors to recognize the local church as God's agent of grace in their midst, because that's what the local church is. While we do have a country office that provides oversight and direction in each of the countries we serve, the delivery system for Compassion's programs at the local level is the local church.

There is a strategic reason for that. Compassion's mission is birthed in the Great Commission. That means we are committed to evangelizing and making disciples. The local church is God's primary vehicle for those tasks.

HEARING THE children sing is one of the most enjoyable experiences for a visiting sponsor or staff member. These vibrant vocalists participate in Compassion's program at a center near Wonji, Ethiopia.

THE CHILDREN'S choir at Ethiopia's Mulu Wongel Student Center in Holeta actively engages in praise and worship.

Compassion seeks local churches that demonstrate a heart to reach the children in their community. We come alongside them with resources, child development strategies, and a vision for transforming children in poverty into productive, fulfilled adults.

Our partners not only resonate with Compassion's goals but also fulfill them with great integrity and creativity. They understand how their community's resources, human or otherwise, can best contribute to the children's well-being. They already know the language of the local children. They have a profound understanding of the challenges those children face and of the potential God has placed within them. And most important, they know each child by name.

Although Compassion is committed to starting early and staying long in the life of a child, the commitment of a local church to children and their families is even greater. That Christian fellowship was there before Compassion ever entered the community and will be there long after Compassion has gone.

That's why Compassion is committed to doing everything possible to prepare our local church partners to administer a well-rounded child development program on their own. It is our goal that they become self-sustaining in this effort, as did our partners in South Korea.

At that point we'll know that children are being valued as they should be. We'll know that the Church has come to share our resolve: to develop children into all that God intended them to be.

TRAIN WE CHILDREN IN WAY WE SHOULD AND WHEN WE ARE OLD WE WILL NOT TURN FROM IT.

MTULEE SISI WATOTO KATIKA NJIA ITUPASAYO NASI HATUTA-IACHA HATA TUTAKAPOKUWA WAZEE.

one child

"WHOEVER WELCOMES ONE OF
THESE LITTLE CHILDREN IN MY
NAME WELCOMES ME; AND
WHOEVER WELCOMES ME DOES
NOT WELCOME ME BUT THE ONE
WHO SENT ME."

Mark 9:37

A YOUNG girl peers through her doorway in a slum of Arusha, Tanzania. The slum was chosen as the location of Tanzania's first Compassion project, Bethel Student Center. Children from this area live in crowded one-room houses without water or electricity, and many suffer from malnutrition, malaria, and water-borne diseases.

Sometimes statistics can be overwhelming.

When you hear about hundreds of thousands of children falling victim to malnutrition, you may feel anxious to help. When you hear that countless numbers are being sold as prostitutes or maimed to become more effective beggars, you might feel compelled to do something. Yet you might not know where to begin or whether anything you could do would actually make a difference.

But what if you knew one of those children by name? What if you had a vital connection that allowed you a unique opportunity to help that child?

It is only at that point, where the big-picture statistics are given human faces, that Jesus called His disciples to accountability. He didn't ask them to solve world hunger. He made no request for sweeping educational reforms. What Jesus asked was far more simple—and much more confrontational: When you find out that someone within your reach is in need, do something to help.

God has placed hundreds of thousands of children within Compassion's reach over the years. But we found that we weren't as effective if we thought of them in terms of hundreds or thousands of children. Instead, we found that approaching our ministry one child at a time was a far more effective strategy.

So day to day, our local staff look for opportunities to treat each child as a valued individual. We encourage each sponsor to affirm his or her sponsored child's dreams for a better life. We believe that is the pattern Jesus taught.

So when we talk about Compassion, we have to go beyond our big-picture statistics. We know that God knows each of His children by name; we believe that we should know the ones He has brought our way by name too.

That's why we love to talk about what we do, one child at a time.

HAVING SUFFERED severe burns to her right hand at the age of one, Dunia Romero has undergone extensive medical treatments with the assistance of Compassion.

one child : d u n i a

One-year-old Dunia Romero of Bolivia, just learning to walk, was stepping tentatively around her small home when she stumbled and fell arm-first into a pot of scalding bathwater. Her pullover sweater kept the steaming water on her hand and arm for several crucial seconds after she was pulled away from the pot.

Following the accident, Dunia's family took her from doctor to doctor in an effort to get her the medical care she needed. The staff at the neighborhood clinic provided only basic first aid, and the doctors in the government-run hospitals were on strike and refused to treat her. A private doctor finally agreed to examine Dunia. Although he waived his fees, the medicines he prescribed were beyond the means of the Romero family, which included two cousins besides Dunia, her seven siblings, and her parents.

In desperation, Dunia's mother turned to the local Compassion project for help. The project staff registered Dunia for child sponsorship and arranged for her to receive a series of operations that would make her hand functional again.

Dunia has one surgery left. Until that takes place, her fingers are being strengthened by an orthopedic glove. She is now able to write her lessons along with her elementary-school classmates—no small miracle, given what she's been through.

a young man after God's own heart

One of Daniel Obrero's earliest memories is of waiting anxiously at the front door to see if his father, a fisherman, would manage to bring home some food for dinner. Daniel also remembers missing many meals and not receiving simple things like toys and candy.

Daniel's five siblings had all left school to support the family, and no one expected that Daniel's future would be any different. However, he committed his life to Jesus Christ when he was nine years old, and he began to pray for a miracle. His prayers were answered one year later when he was sponsored through Compassion. As Daniel says, "Sponsorship really does make a difference. All of a sudden, my life was changed."

With his sponsors' encouragement, Daniel excelled at school and matured both spiritually and socially. After

graduating from high school and completing the child development program, he was selected as one of 42 students from across the Philippines to join the first-ever class of Compassion's Leadership Development Program. For Daniel, who had a great desire to continue his education, the college-tuition assistance and leadership training were yet another answer to prayer.

Daniel chose teaching as his major because, as he says, "that is what Jesus spent most of His time doing." And he more than met the challenge of university studies and the Leadership Development Program. He graduated a year ago with a degree in education and numerous academic and leadership awards.

Despite his hectic schedule and the distractions of young adulthood, Daniel has kept his focus fixed on serving God and others. He takes the pulpit when his pastor is away and also serves as an area missionary in the Filipino province of Abra. Daniel explains, "It is mountainous. It is so far from our place. But my pastor has told me, 'You know, Daniel, you're still young but God is already using you mightily to spread His Word.' "

Because of his passion for service, Daniel's greatest dream was to help other impoverished children through Compassion. He is now employed as a teacher at a Compassion project in his home country, and he says, "I really believe 100 percent that God is using me as an agent of change."

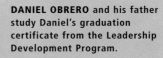

DANIEL OBRERO and his father study Daniel's graduation certificate from the Leadership Development Program.

93

DANIEL OBRERO, now a teacher at a Compassion project, enjoys returning home to fish with his father.

94

one child: diviany

Many families live just one paycheck away from homelessness. When the Brazilian factory that employed Diviany Goncalves Alves's father as a salesman went bankrupt, the Alves family soon found themselves on the street. They moved to a Brazilian city closer to family and are now in the process of getting back on their feet. Diviany's parents still struggle to pay their rent, roughly U.S.$40 a month, and to keep food on the table.

The family's circumstances brought Diviany and one of her two brothers into the Compassion program not long ago. Sponsorship has given them a sense of continuity they have not known for some time. Diviany enjoys school so much that even at age six she is firm about her future profession: she wants to be a teacher.

an entrepreneur for the children

Wilmer Masgo Bravo lives in a shantytown in Peru. Sponsored through Compassion as a child, Wilmer now operates a snack stand a short distance from a school as well as from the student center he once attended.

A diligent young man, Wilmer has paid careful attention to all he's been taught through Compassion. "I learned many things in the Compassion program that have helped me. I especially learned about balanced meals. I learned about the principal kinds of food children need to grow. And I try to apply this knowledge when I sell food to children from this stand.

95

"My mother is the cook for this stand. The foods we sell are inexpensive because the children who buy them are poor, like I was. And if I see children come to school without money for a meal, as I often did as a child, I ask them to come by while their friends aren't watching so I can give them something to eat."

Wilmer is also going to college to get an accounting degree. Someday, he thinks, he might open stands near other schools to give more children access to food they can afford. "My motivation for having my own business is not only to benefit myself but also to benefit others. I see the children's needs, and I would like to meet them through my business."

KRIENGSAK
SIRICHANOKMAS
reads his Bible in
his home near Chiang
Mai, Thailand.

96

one child: kriengsak

A few years ago, Kriengsak Sirichanokmas was hospitalized for a month after suffering injuries from an accidental explosion that occurred while he was helping his uncle to make gunpowder for sale. The event deepened his family's faith and brought about their registration of Kriengsak in a Compassion project not far from his home near Chiang Mai, Thailand.

The sixth of seven children, Kriengsak seems keenly aware of the second chance he's been given, the broad opportunities available in the Compassion program, and his parents' loving and consistent efforts to provide for their family. As he continues through school and the Compassion program, he prays for strength.

"My favorite Bible story is that of Samson," he says. "I want to have a strength like Samson's so I can help my parents work."

one child: james

James Solomon lives with his mother, Rosa Joseph, and a younger sibling in an impoverished neighborhood in Arusha, Tanzania. The family makes its home in a small room owned by Rosa's grandmother.

At age 25, Rosa has already been scarred by two relationships with men who promised to take care of her but abandoned her after she became pregnant. Understandably, Rosa feels as though she has been discarded. She finds her comfort and pride in her son. "My child is very obedient. He listens to me and he obeys me."

Her hope lies in a successful future for her children. That's why she values Compassion sponsorship so highly. "I feel that James being chosen to be part of the project is from Almighty God. . . . I hope that James will be able to build a house someday and that I will live there. I pray that my child will not throw me away when he grows up."

(Top) **JAMES SOLOMON** stands in front of his family's home in Arusha, Tanzania.

(Bottom) Rosa Solomon finds comfort in her son, James.

o n e   c h i l d :   u m a

Children sometimes face social stigmas beyond their control. M. Uma Mageshwari Manoharan's family belongs to a lower caste of the traditional social system in India. As a result, her parents have been undervalued and underemployed all their lives.

But because Uma is a part of the Compassion program, her mother sees great hope for her. She is dreaming dreams for her daughter that were unthinkable in her own generation. "My daughter has no problem concerning caste in the Compassion program. Through Compassion my child will be given a better education. She will study well and grow up to be a doctor or lawyer."

Today, Uma takes pride in helping her mother carry water and care for the new baby in the family. Tomorrow, she may influence her community to open up more opportunities for children from every segment of society.

AT HIS home in a
sprawling Manila slum,
Maximo Resma Jr. studies
his lessons.

one child: maximo

Character development is often the best defense against mean streets. The mother of Maximo Resma Jr. credits Compassion's program with reinforcing the positive Christian values Maximo has been raised with at his home in the Philippines.

"Many of the children here get into vices—some get into drugs and some get into quarrels and fistfights. But Maximo has not. Maximo helps around the house with a lot of things. He takes care of his sister. He runs errands for things we need. He sweeps the house. He studies.

"I pray that Maximo will grow up to be God fearing and to accomplish some of the things we have dreamed of for him: to have a stable job, earn a degree, and maybe even sponsor another child through Compassion himself."

LILIANA MENDEZ shares a letter from her sponsor with her sister.

one child: liliana

As Liliana Mendez was finishing her high school career, a hurricane blew through her Dominican Republic village and demolished her family's modest house. But that didn't deter Liliana from completing her studies. Even as Liliana's family rebuilt from the effects of the hurricane, she was able to stay focused and graduate.

Liliana is determined to use the mathematics skills she has developed over the years to launch a career in computer science. She openly credits her sponsor for giving her ongoing support to do her best. "Whenever my sponsor writes me, he wants to know how I'm doing in school and how I'm doing in church. He always encourages me to keep ahead in my studies."

one child: nelson, yesni, and yaquelin

"Man is born to trouble as surely as sparks fly upward" (Job 5:7). This ancient saying seems an apt description of the lives of Santos Mendez-Merlot and his wife, Ruth Perez. The couple in Guatemala have faced many obstacles while trying to forge a decent life for their children.

Santos works as a farm laborer but can only find occasional employment. Even when he does find work, many jobs pay him just 10 Guatemalan quetzales ($1.25 in U.S. currency) each day, leaving him unable to provide his family with school supplies, medical care, or adequate food.

His wife, Ruth, stays at home and cares for their seven children. Their youngest child was born with severe birth defects and cannot walk, so Ruth spends a great deal of time tending to him. She also maintains a small garden, which she created to be a bright spot in their lives. She explains, "I like to bring my sick boy outside and to show him the flowers and plants. I get joy from this."

After seeing all the needs in this family, the staff of the local Compassion project determined to help in any way they could. They registered three of the children—Nelson, Yesni, and Yaquelin—for sponsorship, and made ongoing medical care available for the youngest child.

Nelson and his twin sisters are now attending school and have begun to build a better future for themselves and their family. Their parents are grateful that the children have this opportunity. Ruth says, "I believe an education is important because it is the greatest heritage parents can give their children, the best legacy they can leave to them."

The family still have their share of troubles, but now they also have hope.

YESNI AND Yaquelin Mendez-Perez take a moment to enjoy the flowers from their garden.

touch and trust

Born to leper parents, Chang Soon Ran was healthy herself. Yet the stigma surrounding the still-misunderstood disease of leprosy caused the state to remove Chang from her home and place her in the New Brightness Christian Children's Home in Inchŏn, South Korea, while she was an infant.

If she had been placed somewhere else, Chang would have been isolated—never touched or played with—because of people's fear of leprosy. But at New Brightness, one of the first Compassion-assisted orphanages in South Korea, Chang received the simple, loving contact she needed from the "mothering ladies" (combined caregivers and nurses).

That care has come full circle. Today, Chang herself is a mothering lady at the children's home, a member of a staff caring for some 60 children. She credits her Compassion sponsor, who was a part of her teenage years, for instilling in her the desire to care for others.

Chang fondly remembers receiving letters, birthday presents, and Christmas gifts from her sponsor. Yet one gift—a substantial cash gift that came with a letter—inspired Chang to reevaluate her own worth and abilities. "I was touched that a sponsor from so far away would trust me so much," Chang recalls, "trust me with such a sum of money."

Today, Chang credits that gift and the gospel with changing her personality. As she realized others considered her to be trustworthy, regardless of her family history, she gained confidence in her own ability to serve. Not only has Chang continued to serve as a mothering lady, but she also supports a child in need through her church's sponsorship program.

"I know the monthly donation can be difficult," Chang says, "but I hope current sponsors will look at me and see me as the positive effect of sponsorship."

one child: amina

With two siblings already grown, nine-year-old Amina Jumanne is one of three children remaining in a single-parent home in Tanzania. Her mother ekes out a living as a vegetable vendor in the local marketplace, bringing home about 1,000 Tanzanian shillings ($1.20 in U.S. currency) a day.

Before Compassion began its work in Tanzania, an education for Amina was simply beyond the means of her family. But now, thanks to Compassion sponsorship, Amina not only attends school but also receives help with her studies and one-on-one attention from the Christian adults at her project. Like any other child, she has her favorite subject (math) and her least favorite (Swahili).

Amina's mother says that her daughter's sponsorship has had other positive effects, beyond just education. "She is very obedient now," she explains, "and she is very good to help with her baby sister. I come back from selling vegetables, and she has cleaned her and changed her and fed her."

As a Compassion-sponsored child, Amina is learning more about the love of God through her relationships with the project staff and her sponsor. And she is on her way to breaking the cycle of poverty her family has known so well.

AMINA JUMANNE proudly displays her school report card along with a picture of her sponsor.

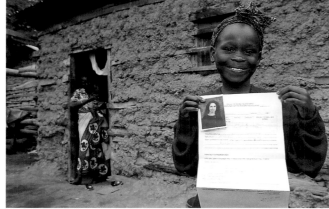

AMINA SEEKS refuge in the arms of her mother. Although Amina is sometimes shy, she is an able student who is in the top 20 percent of her class.

one child: ines

Ines Murga is usually one of her student center's most outgoing children. She often finds herself acting out Bible stories and short plays in front of her peers in Bolivia. But one day Ines was not her energetic self. Her parents noticed that she was lethargic and developing a high fever. Since the Murgas are subsistence farmers, with no extra income for medical treatment, they turned to the Compassion student center she attends for help. The Compassion staff immediately sent Ines to a doctor, who diagnosed a severe case of influenza and started Ines on the road to recovery.

It wasn't the first time Ines received care that she might not have been able to access otherwise. A few years earlier, Ines had broken her hand and received the needed care to retain full use of it—a serious issue for a developing actress and, more important, an active young girl.

DARILIA VAN VOORNEBURG looks over letters from her sponsored child.

sponsorship brings a homecoming to darilia van voorneburg

Darilia van Voorneburg is a professional chef at a large convention center in Holland. Blandive Alcide is a shy, rail-thin girl whose life is being transformed through the Compassion program in her neighborhood in Cap-Haitien, Haiti. You might expect them to have little in common. Yet when Darilia made the 5,000-mile journey from the Netherlands to visit Blandive, her sponsored child, it was a homecoming for her.

Darilia was born in an impoverished community in Cap-Haitien. Her memories from her first few years of life in Cap-Haitien are (perhaps mercifully) few. As a young girl, she was rescued by Catholic nuns who sent her to live in an orphanage in Port-au-Prince. Through arrangements made by some Dutch missionaries in Haiti, Darilia was adopted by Frans and Maria van Voorneburg of the Netherlands.

The child flourished in her new home. In only one year Darilia was becoming fluent in Dutch. Within two years, she had shed the traumas of her past and was becoming a happy-go-lucky child.

Eventually Darilia grew up and became involved in the culinary arts. One Sunday, as she attended church in Apeldoorn, she heard Compassion Nederland President Paul Emans talk about child sponsorship. Darilia approached Paul and asked about the possibility of sponsoring a child from Haiti.

She was linked with Blandive Alcide, who was growing up not far from her own birthplace. They began to correspond—an exchange that fostered Darilia's desire to return to Haiti to visit her sponsored child.

The meeting between the two seemed awkward at first. As with many sponsored children, Blandive wasn't sure what to make of all the attention she received. Darilia was momentarily taken aback by the similarities between Blandive and herself at that age. But they soon found themselves enjoying one another's company and treasuring the time together.

"The relationship is far more personal now," says Darilia. "I have a vivid picture of where Blandive lives and how she lives, and I saw the progress Blandive is making. I'm more committed to sponsorship than ever."

"After seeing Haiti again, I felt blessed and privileged in my own life. I hope, Lord willing, to go back someday and live and work for my people."

113

SIRIPORN SA-O in Chiang Mai, Thailand, connects across half the world with an American named Barbara Bew.

112

Sponsors are the heart of Compassion's outreach to children in need.

Over the last half century, Compassion's ministry has touched the lives of nearly a million children and their families. And each sponsored child in that number has counted on just one sponsor at a time to provide the means for him or her to receive the benefits of Compassion's program. Sometimes for a year, sometimes for many years, Compassion sponsors have faithfully given of their resources to stabilize the lives of children in poverty.

Of course, a sponsor's value to a child (and to Compassion) goes far beyond monetary support. Children look to their sponsors for the encouragement and prayers to make it through everything from a difficult class in school to the loss of a family member. Through letters and pictures, children and sponsors learn about each other. The relationship usually grows into one of the most important for both the sponsor and the child.

One of the best descriptions of a sponsor comes from a child. A few years ago in Colombia, a couple from the United States were addressed as *madrina* and *padrino*. Through a translator, the couple asked their sponsored child, a boy about 10 years old, what the words meant.

The answer was "You know, a godmother or godfather—someone who is close to a family because they are watching out for the child.

"Like you watch out for me."

Steve Giddens first learned about Compassion through 7:22, an interdenominational worship service for single adults in the Atlanta area. He made the decision to sponsor Vladimir Laura of Bolivia. A few years later, on a trip to Bolivia, he got a chance to find out just how much his sponsorship meant to Vladimir and Vladimir's family.

"Even though Vladi's school was closed for summer vacation, the staff considered my visit such a big event that they opened the facility for me to see. All of the children came out to greet me, and I was able to see firsthand the impact that Compassion had on Vladi and the other children.

"After visiting Vladi's school, I was able to see his church and was invited into his home. I was amazed at what a special event it was for Vladi and his family to have me in their small, one-room home. I'm just an ordinary guy, but I was greeted with the honor of a celebrity.

"Vladi referred to me as his padrino, or godfather. The Compassion translator who accompanied me on my visit explained that I was called padrino because I was helping a child grow, even though I wasn't immediate family. I was helping a child see God's hand in his life.

"When I was in Vladi's home, his mother showed me a small photo album where she keeps the few family pictures that she has. Inside the album was a picture I had sent to Vladi, along with every letter that I had written to him. That made me realize how valuable the letters I write are to Vladi and his family.

"At the close of my visit, Vladi's mom insisted that I choose a picture of Vladi from the family picture album to take with me. There were only a few photos of Vladi from the time he was very young; these were of great value to the family. I was reluctant to take one of the few pictures of Vladi that his mother had, but she insisted. I hardly knew what to say—except thank you!

"I had gone on this trip to be a blessing, but I left feeling that I had been blessed far beyond what I could ever give.

"I am thankful to Compassion for allowing me—as a sponsor or padrino—to be a part of its eternal impact on Vladi and children like him all over the world."

lois pierce closes the distance between
herself and her sponsored child

Lois Pierce is a former missionary and church planter whose work focused on the state of Ceará in Brazil. Some time after Lois returned to Pennsylvania from Brazil, she decided to sponsor a child from Ceará. Compassion linked Lois with Luzifabia de Maria, a grade-school student at a Compassion-assisted school in Fortaleza, Ceará's capital.

"When I went to visit Luzifabia a year ago, we hugged and didn't let go," Lois recalls. "Then Luzifabia showed me around the elementary school she'd attended, her grandmother's house, and then her mother's house, which is two rooms with a chicken coop attached. Luzifabia lives there with her mother, stepfather, and five other children.

"Not long into our visit at Luzifabia's home, she pulled out an envelope containing my picture and every letter I'd ever sent. I quickly found out that her family knew about me too. Luzifabia's mother was thrilled to see me, and we had a warm, memorable visit together.

"Sponsorship is making a much bigger difference for Luzifabia than I'd thought it could. Her family is able to buy chickens because my Compassion support relieves the economic strain of Luzifabia's school costs.

"Since the visit, Luzifabia no longer seems so far away. I can imagine her in her surroundings as I pray. When I look at her picture on my desk at work, my mind travels to Fortaleza, and I am reminded of how much Luzifabia and I both have to be thankful for."

There are few things like a firsthand visit to show that sponsorship works. Italian sponsors Tatiana and Giulio Romagnoli already sponsored five children when they visited this South India project. Since that trip, the Romagnolis have decided to sponsor another eight Indian children.

Lorraine Smith and her sponsored child, Lourdes Analy Oliva, enjoy a break from the Guatemalan sunshine during their December 1995 visit.

Roy and Margie Thompson traveled to Machola, Ecuador, in September 1996 and personally saw the difference their sponsorship of Nerida Isabel Sarmiento had made.

Canadian sponsor Andrew Boone enjoys a day with his sponsored child at her home in Ecuador. Whenever possible, Compassion tries to arrange a home visit so the sponsor can better understand the child's everyday circumstances.

their trip to Thailand, Dennis and Lorraine Gleeson met both sponsored child, Wutinun Chuchum, and his mother. Sponsorship often affects a child's parents almost as much as the child.

Angelica Garcia greets her sponsors, Howard and May Cook, in her "Sunday best" traditional Guatemalan dress.

"After meeting Alejandro, I realized that each one of us can help build a better world with little acts of love." Italian gospel singer Aurelio Pitino was clearly a hit with his sponsored child, Alejandro Jose, in Tegucigalpa, Honduras.

Karen Judenhagen and her sponsored child, Jhon Mejia Arias, enjoy time together in Ecuador.

Sonia Estela Alvares Salinas was all smiles when her sponsor, LuAnn Hearn, visited her in El Salvador in 1996.

Kamala Devi Thoguru was only six when Keith Strong's family became her sponsors in 1986. After years of building their relationship across the miles, Keith finally was able to travel to India to meet Kamala in 1995.

When Paige Burgess traveled to Thailand in 1997, her sponsored child, Artit Winekwanarom, relished the opportunity to climb into her lap for a little food and a lot of attention.

Missy Kirk and Maadugula Praveena enjoyed a beautiful day—and the pleasure of each

Doug Davis made the trip to the Dominican Republic to visit his sponsored child, ...is E. Corporam Rodriguez, in January 1999.

Alfred Bessie joined with his family in Indonesia to welcome his sponsor, Mike Gagan, in November 1995.

The relationship between a sponsor and child often bridges t... distance between hemispheres, as Bob Edwards of the Unite... States found when he visited Freddy Colque, his sponsored ch... in Bolivia.

The experience was even more spectacular than the scenery: Danny

Joaquin Yumbo was thrilled that his sponsor, Hae-jin Kim, made the trip all the way from Canada to Ecuador just to meet him.

"Sponsorship made such a difference in my life," says Saroj Sami, once a Compassion-sponsored child in Fiji. Saroj now lives with her husband, Veeran, and daughter, Monisha, in Australia. The Sami family sponsors four children through Compassion.

Two families celebrate the positive impact of Compassion sponsorship: Peter and Dawn Gudel brought their children to meet the Gudel's sponsored child, Berinese Yvorte, and her family on an August 1997 journey to the Dominican Republic.

February 1999: When a sponsor visits his sponsored child, it's a happy day for both parties. Smiles were everywhere as Jose Helu and his sponsored child, Melissa Jimenez, met in the Dominican Republic.

March 1998: Susan Strong and her sponsored child, Roberto Ramos Cifuentes, spent part of the day at a restaurant enjoyed by kids all over the world, including Guatemala.

Barbara Bew and her sponsored child, Siriporn Sa-o, in Siriporn's home in Thailand, where Barbara has just presented her with several gifts to celebrate their time together.

Deb Sheehan gives an introductory photography lesson to Victor Hernandez, her sponsored child, during her trip to meet Victor in Ecuador.

New Zealand's Rule family made a young Thai girl's day—and gave her memories for a lifetime—with their visit to Pinamat Ja-Ue.

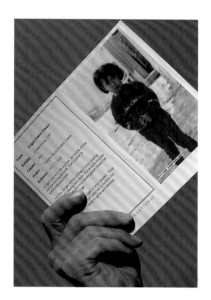

one cause

REBECCA ST. JAMES talks
with young volunteers
before a concert at
Kingdom Bound Festival.

AT THE CLOSE of a Compassion Sunday event, speaker and humorist Ken Davis visits with people signing up to become Compassion sponsors.

"SPEAK UP FOR THOSE WHO CANNOT
SPEAK FOR THEMSELVES, FOR THE
RIGHTS OF ALL WHO ARE DESTITUTE.
SPEAK UP AND JUDGE FAIRLY;
DEFEND THE RIGHTS OF THE POOR
AND NEEDY."

Proverbs 31:8–9

You need faith and perseverance to speak up for those who have no voice. There's no guarantee that those you talk with will understand what you're saying, much less share your passion for the cause. Sometimes people respond immediately. More often, there's no visible evidence that they heard you.

But the volunteers, speakers, and music artists who speak up for the children of Compassion keep trying because they have a sense of how God Himself values the children of the destitute. They understand that God values impoverished children for who they are now, not simply for the adults they could become.

They share that message with others in a variety of ways. Members of the Volunteer Network staff sponsorship sign-up tables at festivals and concerts, lead Bible studies, and make presentations to church groups on Compassion Sunday (among other things). Christian music artists and speakers use their public platforms to promote Compassion sponsorship to their audiences.

Here are just a few of the people who have taken on the cause of little ones who cannot yet speak for themselves. They represent a host of sponsors, volunteers, and noted personalities who have come to value children of poverty in the way that God does—and who encourage others to do the same.

REBECCA ST. JAMES believes that her sponsorship of Anusha and her work with Compassion have fulfilled her childhood dream of working with children in need. *Photo (left) by Michelle Brown.*

rebecca st. james: spreading the dream

"When I was a little girl," recalls Christian musician Rebecca St. James, "I wanted to have a home for the poor in inner-city Sydney so they could get washed up, have a meal and a bed, and pay little or nothing for it. I especially wanted to help needy children. Compassion is a way I can fulfill that dream and spread that dream to others.

"I saw Compassion's work firsthand when I went to Calcutta, India, with my mom. In Calcutta I was able to visit Anusha, the child I sponsored.

"Our visit to Anusha's house really sums up what Compassion is about. The whole family shared one bed. They didn't have much, but they took delight in what they had. And Anusha was thrilled that I sponsored her. The defining moment came when her mother asked if she could pray for me and ask God's blessing on my singing. The gratitude and grace of Anusha and her family were a response, in part, to how Compassion was affecting their lives.

"I could see then how sponsorship affected not only Anusha but also her family and her community. I visited Calcutta Immanuel School in the neighborhood. The children had prepared a performance for us and sang Christian songs in English. I sensed that these kids had a hope, a future, and a purpose for living.

"My involvement with Compassion has expanded my worldview. It also expands the worldview of those who come to my concerts. Compassion offers them a practical way to share the love of Jesus with some very precious children."

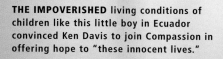

THE IMPOVERISHED living conditions of children like this little boy in Ecuador convinced Ken Davis to join Compassion in offering hope to "these innocent lives."

ken davis: bringing about change

Comedian and inspirational speaker Ken Davis offers the gospel with a smile to audiences throughout the United States. Over the years, they've grown accustomed to Ken's winsome insights and well-developed humor. They've also listened to Ken's heart as he's shared about his face-to-face visits with Compassion-sponsored children.

"I took the opportunity to travel to Ecuador to see Compassion's child development ministry in action. Wherever Compassion had a project, I witnessed joy in the midst of overwhelming poverty. I was so overcome with the difference that sponsorship can make in the life of a child that I joined forces with Compassion to help bring hope to these innocent lives.

"It wasn't the sight of the poverty that changed my life; it was the evidence of how effectively lives can be changed with a little sacrifice on our part. I have seen the smiles and heard the testimonies of children who were without hope but then found joy because someone decided to sponsor them.

"My life was changed forever when I encountered children living in abject poverty in Ecuador. But the good news is that their lives have been changed by the love and generosity of sponsors."

MICHAEL W. SMITH and his family
sponsored Gavi for a dozen years,
watching her grow from a little
girl into a confident young woman.
Photo (above) by Gaylon Wampler.
Photo (right) archive photo.

michael w. smith: somehow God miraculously put us together

Comparing his life growing up in a small West Virginia town to the lives of children he's seen in Compassion projects, Michael W. Smith notes some similarities: "Kids are kids. Kids everywhere seem to spend time playing in the streets. We do a lot of the same things—throwing rocks, throwing the ball, anything to create a game.

"But the similarities end when poverty is added to the situation. I've seen kids who are struggling just to survive nutritionally.

"The first time I came face-to-face with that reality, it was overwhelming. I couldn't process all the sights, sounds, and smells I was experiencing. I had gone from holding my own kids, safe and healthy in my own home, to holding a baby overseas who was probably not going to live much longer.

"I didn't intend to speak out for Compassion at first. I simply wanted to sponsor a child. I went to Ecuador, and this little girl named Gavi latched onto me for the whole time I was there. I sponsored her. Then as I went to several nearby projects and saw the quality of the work, that solidified everything for me.

"I considered it a privilege to be involved in Gavi's life. During the dozen years that I sponsored her, I watched her mature from a young girl into a young woman. And I found her to be, quite honestly, an extraordinary person. She was gifted and demonstrated a lot of leadership skills.

"Probably the most miraculous part of Gavi's story was her spiritual transformation and the ripple effect that had on her family. Because of sponsorship, Gavi came to know the Lord. Now her grandmother and grandfather have come to know the Lord too. So have her cousins and nephews and aunts and uncles. . . . In all, 23 people in her family have come to faith in Christ because of one sponsorship.

"Gavi's dad has been gone since she was two. And you know what? I think that I've been a daddy to her. She has said that every time we've parted. And she's cried. We've both cried.

"I'm glad that I got to play that part in her life. I'm glad that I was born in this day and age and that somehow God miraculously put us together. I think it was a God thing.

"And because it's a God thing, it's exciting to be the one to tell 15,000 concertgoers about Compassion for the first time. It's exciting talking with my friends about Compassion too. I love talking about Compassion."

a decade of difference

Sponsorship makes all the difference for volunteers because they see the difference it makes for the children they sponsor. Just ask Kenneth Stevenson.

"Every time I have the opportunity to speak out on behalf of poor and needy children around the world," he says, "I always share my story about Fredy.

"In January 1987 I traveled on a missions trip with a group from my church to Lima, Peru. While I was there, I met Fredy Perez, the child I had just begun to sponsor through Compassion. I had a friend videotape my visit at Fredy's home.

"When I returned to the States, I called Compassion to thank them for setting up that visit and to tell them how impressed I was with their work. It was then that I heard about the new Volunteer Network and decided to become a part of it.

"For the next decade I showed the video of my visit with Fredy whenever possible. The impact that video had on my audiences was tremendous. Over the years, over 150 children around the world were sponsored with the help of the video.

"Ten years after my first visit with Fredy, I went back to Lima and saw him again. I had our meeting videotaped and compiled the new footage with the tape of our first meeting. The combined video shows the impact Compassion has had on Fredy—how he has grown up into a healthy, intelligent young man who is a productive member of his family and community.

"Fredy is studying business administration now at the University of Peru. The last time we were together, he introduced me to his fiancée and asked if I would be best man at their wedding.

"I know the Lord will continue to use Fredy's story to help many other children through the ministry of Compassion."

glad: a desire to be different

Glad is a musical group known for its tight harmonies and wide-ranging repertoire. And the harmony between Glad and Compassion has blessed many hundreds of children and sponsors for over 15 years.

During this time, Glad members have made it a point to visit Compassion's work firsthand whenever possible. Their journeys have taken them to Africa, Asia, Central America, and South America. Don Nalle, one of the original members, says, "We are always moved when we visit Compassion projects."

Such a visit to Bolivia in 1994 moved Glad's Don Pardoe to sponsor Roberto Arcane. "Roberto was only eight years old then and was very shy compared to the other children we met on the trip," Don remembers. "I was so overwhelmed by the poverty I saw in Bolivia that I didn't want to leave Roberto there. But I knew that through Compassion sponsorship, he would be given many opportunities. So in reality I wasn't leaving Roberto; I was leaving him with hope.

"Over the years, I've seen Roberto grow in many ways. I can tell from his confident smile in the pictures I receive that he isn't a shy little boy anymore. And I can tell from his letters that he isn't willing to give in to the hopelessness around him—he has a desire to be different."

more than they dreamed

Jeff and Julie Patterson sponsored their first child six months prior to their wedding. Jeff was so passionate about Compassion sponsorship that he dreamed of adding a sponsorship for every anniversary they celebrated.

For their first year of marriage they sponsored one child, and in their second year of marriage they sponsored a second child. They hoped to commemorate their golden anniversary by sponsoring their 50th child. But then their own children were born, their money was needed in other places, and their plans for sponsoring dozens of children seemed, well, impractical. . . .

Now Jeff and Julie Patterson have been married for 15 years, and God has used them to bless even more children than they had dreamed. They have sponsored eight children themselves and have found sponsors for nearly 300 others through their roles as Compassion volunteers.

What has motivated them to keep sponsoring and speaking out for children over the long haul? According to Julie, the answer is relationships. She explains, "The relationships we share with our sponsored children continually motivate us to be a voice for those who are waiting for a sponsor."

The Pattersons' relationship with their second sponsored child, Taciana, was a life-changing experience for them. Jeff and Julie began sponsoring Taciana when she was six years old and exchanged numerous letters with her as she grew up. Finally, when Taciana was 17 years old, they had the opportunity to visit her in Brazil.

Julie comments, "We realized from her letters that we were important in her life, but it was overwhelming to realize *how* important. She had come to believe, 'I matter, my life is worthwhile, because these people I haven't even met believe in me and are investing in my future.' "

Jeff and Julie Patterson have always dreamed big. But God has used the Pattersons to bless children's lives much more than they had ever dreamed.

orchestrated by God

Ephesians 2:10 says, "We are God's workmanship, created in Christ Jesus to do good works, which God prepared in advance for us to do." Volunteer Jeff Bradshaw knows from experience that this is true.

"In 1986 my wife and I traveled to Mexico City," Jeff recalls. "I had been to some of the islands in the Caribbean before this trip and had been able to ignore the plight of the poor. But on this trip I took notice of the people. One image that stuck in my mind was that of whole families with their children begging on the city streets.

"Within a year of that trip, I saw a Compassion ad on television and sponsored a child from Mexico. For the first year I wondered if this program really worked or if it was some sort of band-aid solution. But as time went on, I was amazed to see what God was doing in the children's lives.

"Then in 1997, I joined the Volunteer Network. And I have seen God make the right times and places for me to share Compassion's ministry with others.

"One example of this happened not long ago at a Promise Keepers gathering in Orlando, Florida. Just as I sat down in the arena, the person on stage requested that all the men pray for one another. I immediately found myself praying with two men whom I had met literally seconds before. We had a powerful time of prayer. Afterward, the men asked me if I had come with anyone. I told them that I was attending the gathering as a Compassion volunteer, and I briefly shared about the ministry.

"Later on during the event, one of the two men sought me out at the Compassion table and sponsored two children. He told me that the prayer time we had shared together had moved him and that he felt strongly led to become a sponsor.

"It's this kind of personal contact, orchestrated by God, that fills me with enthusiasm for promoting the cause of children."

(Left) **PHIL KEAGGY** was an early fixture in the Compassion artists' roster and has been an active sponsor for two decades.

(Below) Phil Keaggy and Randy Stonehill often performed together in the 1980s. They came together for "Who Will Save the Children?," still one of the most compelling songs ever written on behalf of the children of Compassion. *Archive photo.*

phil keaggy: full of gratitude

"Three times, my wife and I were expecting children and lost those babies at birth," says Christian music artist Phil Keaggy. "By the time Compassion first approached us, Bernadette and I had been blessed with Alicia, a healthy, beautiful child. We realized how precious children were. And when I came to understand what Compassion was about, and that I could be useful to Compassion's ministry as a musician, I was interested in the opportunity.

"Compassion gave me the chance to go overseas and see the work for myself. Visits like that open your heart and make your whole system sensitive to the needs of children. They also make you grateful to God for the answers He provides through Compassion—the relief and the hope.

"We sponsored Edrick, who lives in Haiti, through elementary school and high school. He ended up studying at the police academy and finding a good job. More important, he grew up with the love of Jesus, learning the things of the Kingdom and learning how to be a good and faithful steward of what God has blessed him with.

"The letters of the children we sponsored after Edrick would just melt our hearts. For example, the letters Bernadette and I received from our sponsored child in the Philippines, Arlene Tempess, were very articulate and full of her love and appreciation for us as sponsors.

"I think people would be surprised at how full of gratitude the children Compassion reaches really are. They don't take a smile for granted. They don't take an embrace for granted. If you send them a gift, they're anxious to write you back immediately and thank you. Or they'll tell you how the gift has blessed their family, or how they were able to buy something useful with it. They are joyful and overflowing with gratitude.

"If what few words I say have encouraged people to get involved with Compassion, I hope they have discovered how much sponsorship enriches their own life, just as it is an enormous blessing in a child's life. It's really worth doing. It's something you never regret."

Randy Stonehill and his wife, Sandy, began sponsoring Dina Pierre in 1983. Left in a Haitian orphanage shortly after birth, Dina found a relationship with Jesus Christ and a sense of family because of the Stonehills' sponsorship.

"I have learned that my mother wandered all over the streets with me when I was a baby," Dina says. "But God had a plan for me. He used someone to take me to the orphanage and then sent a family for me: the Stonehills."

Randy agrees with Dina. "I believe that our sponsorship has given Dina a real sense of family connection. I tell my friends that Dina is a treasure from God, a spiritually adopted daughter who has taught me more about true faith than almost anyone else in my life.

"A few years ago, Dina and I spent a whole day together in the Compassion Haiti office. I was overwhelmed by the 'fragrance of Christ' that permeated Dina. Singing is Dina's favorite hobby, so we sang her favorite hymns together—she in French and me in English. As we sang, she gently rested her head on my shoulder, like I was her father. . . . It was one of the greatest moments of my life. I was humbled to realize that God had allowed me a small part in the glorious work that He was doing in her life."

Dina is deeply aware of the Stonehills' impact on her life. "My life was changed because of sponsorship. I would never have been able to attend school without sponsorship. Compassion's program and the Stonehills led me to know Christ. What more can I say? I have one Father in Jesus—God—and one father in faith—Randy Stonehill."

RANDY STONEHILL enjoys a day with his "spiritually adopted daughter" in Haiti. *Archive photo.*

tony campolo: how we treat the poor is how we treat Jesus

Sociologist and speaker Tony Campolo has been a pioneer in bringing suburban Christians face-to-face with poverty in the United States and abroad for over two decades. His consistent biblical references, edgy humor, and ability to give the issues a human face have made Tony a sought-after headliner at festivals and conferences since the late 1970s.

Most of that time, Tony, a Compassion sponsor himself, has made a point of encouraging his audiences to consider sponsoring a child. "Compassion sponsorship brings Jesus' passion for children together with His call to remember the poor.

"We live in a culture where ignoring both the poor and Jesus is the norm. But Jesus Himself warned that how we treat the poor is exactly how we treat Him. If we want to be true disciples of Jesus Christ, then watching out for 'the least' of Jesus' brothers and sisters

has to be a high priority for us.

"In fact, the only detailed account of Judgment Day that Jesus offers is the account of the sheep and the goats. It's in the 25th chapter of Matthew.

"I find it curious that in separating the two groups as they head toward their eternal destinies, no questions are asked about classic Christian orthodoxy. The issues that we've divided the church over in the last 2,000 years are missing completely. Instead, the question that sorts out those who are in a relationship with God and those who aren't is this: 'What did you do with the sick, the naked, the hungry, the thirsty, the imprisoned?'

"Jesus was clear that our relationship with Him, or lack of it, would show in how we treated those in need. Compassion sponsorship is one way we can live that relationship out."

TONY CAMPOLO'S
a welcome visitor
to these children at
a student center
in Ecuador.

finding a place to serve

Susan Sande had already touched many young lives as a mother and as a speech therapist in the Fond du Lac, Wisconsin, public schools. But she wanted to do more.

"Before I knew about Compassion's Volunteer Network," she recalls, "I spent months asking God to give me direction as to what He wanted me to do. Then one day I saw in a mailing that I could apply to be a Compassion volunteer. I knew immediately that God had answered my prayer.

139

"I had sponsored Lina Milena Mena Munoz in Colombia for years. I had prayed for her, written to her, and loved her for years. I'd seen the incredible, godly young lady she had become. I had seen that I had helped to change her life dramatically. I knew how intensely God loved this one child, and I knew I had ministered to Him by helping Lina.

"I could make a difference for hundreds more children by becoming a volunteer. So the choice was obvious.

"Not long after joining the Volunteer Network, I went on a trip to Thailand with other volunteers. I saw the heart of Jesus in the way the Compassion staff ministered to the children there. I held the little girls we now sponsor and talked to the teachers and director of the project they attend, and I knew they were being cared for by the best staff and the best organization.

"Each time I help a sponsor find a child to love, pray for, and support, I think of that teenage girl in Thailand or that little boy in India and of how children like that will feel when they find out someone has chosen to sponsor them."

For Susan, loving and serving children like these have brought renewed vitality to her own relationship with God. "The more compassion you give God's children, the more He fills your heart."

(Above) **FOR MANY** years, Amy Grant
has witnessed the profound impact
Compassion's ministry has on
sponsors and sponsored children.
Her visits to Compassion projects
have strengthened her commitment
to help children escape the bonds
of poverty.

(Below) Amy cherished the time she
spent with Luis, the young boy she
sponsors in Guatemala. *Photos by
Gaylon Wampler.*

amy grant: a prayer from luis

The world is changed as children—and sponsors—are impacted through sponsorship.
Ask Amy Grant, who has been a Compassion sponsor and spokesperson for years.

"My children and I were deeply moved when we visited Luis, one of the boys we
sponsor in Guatemala," Amy said. "We became very fond of Luis and his mother.

"Before we left, they asked to pray with us. His mother led. Then Luis wrapped his
arms around me. He prayed that God would make all my music, and that God would bless
all the songs I sang so I could continue to be his sponsor.

"Luis was nine. He'd probably never heard the radio, much less a song I'd sung. That
prayer completely wiped me out.

"Sponsorship is one of those things that make a profound difference years down the
road, in our lives as well as those of the children."

geoff moore: insights into children

The intense, high-energy musician his audiences applaud at a concert is only one part of who Geoff Moore is. Geoff is also a committed Christian, a devoted husband and father, an advocate for impoverished children . . . and a Compassion sponsor. During the hours he invests in prayer, he often intercedes for Klever Mendoza, the 12-year-old from Ecuador whom he and his family have sponsored over the years.

The Moores' sponsorship has accomplished much in Klever's life. As Klever himself expressed in a recent letter to Geoff, "Without a sponsor, I wouldn't have medical treatments. I wouldn't have help in general. Through being sponsored, I have come to know the Lord Jesus Christ."

Being both a father and a sponsor has given Geoff greater insights into children and the everyday challenges they face. "I've learned as a dad and as a sponsor that children from different cultures have a lot in common, even though the circumstances they face may be radically different.

"Klever's a great example. When Klever shows up on the playground for soccer, all the intensity and focus you'd see in any 12-year-old athlete come right to the surface. But the everyday circumstances that he has to deal with to get to the playground are way different than what most of us in the States could ever imagine.

"My prayer for Klever is that he'll learn to approach his relationship with Jesus Christ with the same intensity he applies to soccer."

one challenge

145

AFTER ATTENDING the Compassion-assisted Emmanuel School in Chennai, India, Nalini Arumugam settles onto the floor to do her homework.

IF YOU SPEND YOURSELVES IN BEHALF OF THE
HUNGRY AND SATISFY THE NEEDS OF THE OPPRESSED,
THEN YOUR LIGHT WILL RISE IN THE DARKNESS, AND
YOUR NIGHT WILL BECOME LIKE THE NOONDAY.

Isaiah 58:10

STUDENTS ATTENDING the Nakatete Child Development Center near Masaka, Uganda, start their early morning trek to the center. Many students walk about a half an hour each way.

Now you have seen the tremendous needs of children in our world and the unparalleled opportunities to transform their lives. What do you intend to do about it?

This question, which Everett Swanson struggled to answer 50 years ago, is a question for each one of us. The Bible makes it clear that the poor will always be with us. And it also makes it clear that we are to spend our time, our resources, and even ourselves to help them. So what do you intend to do about it? Will you spend yourself on behalf of children in need?

War visits children in Rwanda. Violence shatters the lives of teenagers in inner-city Chicago. They all need someone to help them wade through the aftermath.

One child sniffs glue with his friends on a street in Brazil; another lights a joint in an alley in New Jersey. Isn't there a common pain?

One child struggles with math in Uganda; another strains to read at grade level on a reservation in New Mexico. Couldn't they both use tutors?

Then what do you intend to do about it?

One of the most effective things you can do for children is pray. This book provides scores of starting points so you can pray for the needs of impoverished children. You might focus on the children pictured or the specific issues and circumstances highlighted. Who knows what your targeted prayer can accomplish? "The prayer of a righteous man is powerful and effective" (James 5:16).

Sponsorship is another vital answer for many children around the world. You've seen how a small investment of time and money can have an immense impact on a child in need, how a sponsor's influence can transform a neglected little one into a confident child of God. That can be *your* impact, *your* influence.

151

A GIRL rests a Bible on her head while waiting in line for school supplies at a project in Kampala, Uganda.

Impoverished children closer to home also need your time and attention. Tutoring is crucial to the success of immigrant students whose parents work long hours for minimum wage. Mentoring can change the futures of children whose horizons are limited by poverty. Teaching Sunday school can impact eternity in neighborhoods where gang violence and broken families are the norm.

You can multiply your impact by speaking out on behalf of children in poverty. God can use you to open others' eyes to the needs of children and the biblical mandate to care for them. Sharing this book with your friends and family is an easy way to begin.

The key to Compassion has always been caring people reaching beyond themselves to help children in need. The challenge is to invest yourself—whether as an intercessor, a sponsor, a volunteer, or an advocate—to bring the love of God to little ones who live in poverty. That kind of investment can change the world for countless children.

155

EVERETT SWANSON PROVED THAT ONE PERSON CAN HAVE AN INCREDIBLE IMPACT. TODAY, THAT PERSON IS YOU.

epilogue

156

BAIK EI SUN holds up an oil portrait of Everett Swanson. The portrait hangs in
Baik's office at the senior citizens' home he directs in Suwon City, South Korea.

Reverend Baik Ei Sun looks out over a sea of smiling octogenarians at the home for the aged he directs in Suwon City, South Korea. He is director and chief administrator of the Social Welfare Juridical Person Central Home for the Aged, a care facility for 75 elderly people who have no other means of support.

Baik can't help breaking out in a grin himself. "This is what it's all about," he says. "This is my way of paying back what Compassion has done in my life: helping others in need."

Baik knows the ins and outs of life in a group home from personal experience. He grew up in a Compassion-assisted orphanage, having lost both parents to the Korean conflict.

Everett Swanson and Baik met at the orphanage in Masan in 1957, when Baik was a teenager. Everett sponsored Baik and paid his way through seminary, ensuring that Baik would receive the sort of formal theological training Everett himself had gone without. Their relationship flourished as the two frequently exchanged letters until Everett's death in 1965.

To this day, Baik remembers Everett's words of encouragement: "Study hard, study hard. Get ordained and become a pastor!" And so he did. In addition to his role at the seniors' home, Baik is an associate pastor at Suwon Central Baptist Church, home to one of the largest congregations in Korea.

Baik calls himself "the fruit of Compassion." He still recounts from the pulpit his experiences as a Compassion-sponsored child. And he offers a message to children who are sponsored. "Grow up to be faithful people who care for others in need. Keep good faith and be thankful for your sponsors."

Baik certainly has taken his own advice. Today, he represents a generation of Christians in Korea who are working to bring the ministry of Compassion full circle. He and other Korean believers are exploring the necessary steps to bring Compassion to South Korea again, only this time they desire to become Compassion sponsors themselves.

Not long ago, Baik needed a new building to expand the seniors' home. The facility was built and dedicated to the memory of Everett Swanson. But Baik also recognizes that he is as much a monument to Everett as the building is.

As Baik says, "The lifetime impact on me is Everett Swanson's dream realized."

1. United Nations Children's Fund [UNICEF], *The State of the World's Children 2000* (New York, 2000), 13, quoting World Bank, "World Bank Warns Global Poverty Fight Failing, Unveils Enhanced Poverty Strategy" in news release 2000/059/S, September 30, 1999, 4.

2. United Nations High Commissioner for Refugees [UNHCR], *Refugees* 1, no. 122 (Geneva, 2001), 7.

3. World Health Organization [WHO], "Child Malnutrition," fact sheet no. 119, November 1996, retrieved October 22, 2001 <http://www.who.int/inf-fs/en/fact119.html>.

4. Gordon Cook, *Manson's Tropical Diseases* (London: Saunders, 1998), 239.

5. UNICEF, *The State of the World's Children 2001* (New York, 2001), 85.

6. UNICEF, *State of the World's Children 2000,* 56.

7. Ibid., 56–57.

8. UNICEF, *State of the World's Children 2001,* 89.

9. UNICEF, *State of the World's Children 2000,* 30, quoting Joint UN Programme on HIV/AIDS and WHO, *AIDS Epidemic Update: December 1998* (Geneva: UNAIDS/WHO, 1998), 3.

10. UNICEF, *State of the World's Children 2000,* 30, quoting Ruth Leger Sivard, *World Military and Social Expenditures 1996* (Washington, D.C.: World Priorities, 1996), 18.

11. UNICEF, *State of the World's Children 2000,* 30, quoting Joint UN Programme on HIV/AIDS, *Facts and Figures 1999* (Geneva, February 1999), 1.

12. UNICEF, *State of the World's Children 2000,* 24, quoting International Labour Organization, "ILO Concludes 87th Conference with Adoption of New Instruments against Child Labour," *World of Work* 30 (July 1999): 2.

13. Ibid.

14. UNHCR, *Refugees* 1, no. 122 (Geneva, 2001), 7.

15. UNICEF, *State of the World's Children 2000,* 20, 24, quoting International Labour Organization, "ILO Concludes 87th Conference," 6.

16. UNICEF, *State of the World's Children 2000,* 24, 28, quoting Stockholm International Peace Research Institute, *SIPRI Yearbook 1999* (Oxford: Oxford University Press, 1999), 2.

17. UNICEF, *State of the World's Children 2000,* 28, quoting International Committee of the Red Cross, *Landmines Must Be Stopped: ICRC Overview 1998* (Geneva, May 1998), 16.

18. Amnesty International, "Humankind Owes the Child 'the Best It Has to Give,' " AI index 76/014/1999, September 1, 1999, retrieved October 22, 2001 <http://web.amnesty.org/ai.nsf/index/act760141999>.